The Anarchists in the Russian Revolution

DOCUMENTS OF REVOLUTION
General Editor: Heinz Lubasz

The Anarchists
in the Russian Revolution

EDITED BY PAUL AVRICH

CORNELL UNIVERSITY PRESS
Ithaca, New York

To the Memory of Peter Kropotkin
on the Fiftieth Anniversary of His Death

FRONTISPIECE: Group of anarchists
released from prison to attend the
funeral of Kropotkin on 13 February
1921, the last occasion on which the
black flag of anarchism was paraded
through the streets of Moscow.

Picture research by Alla Weaver

First published 1973 by Cornell University
Press.

This edition is not for sale in the United
Kingdom and British Commonwealth.

International Standard Book Number 0–8014–0780–X
Library of Congress Catalog Card Number 72–13386

Printed in Great Britain.

Contents

PART THREE: WORKERS' CONTROL

PART FOUR: SOCIAL REVOLUTION

PART FIVE: THE OCTOBER INSURRECTION

PART SIX: CIVIL WAR

Caricature of 1848 showing Pierre-Joseph Proudhon (1809–65) attacking the property concept. From Proudhon, a seminal figure in the anarchist tradition, the Russian anarchists derived some of their distrust for centralization and politicians and a rudimentary conception of workers' control.

Introduction

ALTHOUGH the vision of a stateless society without coercion or exploitation dates back to ancient times, the greatest moments of anarchism in action occurred in our own century, during the Russian Revolution and the Spanish Civil War. The Revolution of 1917 was the first occasion when anarchists attempted to put their theories into practice on a broad scale. By means of 'direct action' – expropriation, workers' control, guerrilla warfare, free communes – they endeavoured to build a new society on libertarian lines and to make their stateless vision a reality.

The anarchist movement embraced a fascinating and sometimes contradictory variety of groups and individuals – Communists and Syndicalists, pacifists and terrorists, idealists and adventurers – whose wide range of theory and practice was never more apparent than during the Russian Revolution. To capture the spirit of the movement during this remarkable, if ultimately tragic, moment of its history is the object of the present volume. Through their articles and manifestos, speeches and resolutions, letters and diaries, poems and songs, the story of the anarchists in the Revolution and Civil War is told by the participants themselves in their own words. No secondary materials have been used. I have drawn exclusively from primary sources which directly convey the nature of anarchist thought and action, and which therefore constitute a living record of the movement. The best-known figures – Kropotkin and Makhno, Maksimov and Gordin, Shapiro and Volin – are of course well represented in this collection. But to give some feeling of the grass-roots movement I have tried to include a broad sampling of documents from the rank and file – workers and peasants as well as students and intellectuals. Each selection or group of related selections is preceded by a brief introductory note placing it in its historical context and explaining any obscure references. At the outset, however, a general introduction is necessary to provide a picture of the movement as a whole.

THE FEBRUARY REVOLUTION

'The urge to destroy is also a creative urge.' Michael Bakunin, the father of Russian anarchism, wrote these famous words in 1842, and his disciples yearned ever after for a social revolution that would sweep away the tsarist order and usher in the stateless millennium. In February 1917 this long-cherished dream seemed at last to be coming true. When rebellion erupted in Petrograd and brought the monarchy to dust, the anarchists hailed it as the spontaneous upheaval which Bakunin had forecast some seventy-five years before (Documents 1, 2). Although they played only a small part in the rising, which was essentially a spontaneous affair, neither organized nor led by any political group, the complete breakdown of authority convinced them that the golden age had arrived, and they threw themselves into the task of eliminating what remained of the state and transferring the land and the factories to the common people.

In a matter of weeks anarchist federations were created in Petrograd and Moscow with the aim of transforming the twin capitals into egalitarian communes modelled on an idealized image of the Paris Commune of 1871, an event consecrated in anarchist legend. 'Through a Social Revolution to the Anarchist Commune' was their watchword – a revolution designed to remove government and property, prisons and barracks, money and profits, and then to inaugurate a stateless society founded on the voluntary cooperation of free individuals. 'Hail anarchy! Make the parasites, rulers and priests – deceivers all – tremble!'[1]

As the revolution gathered momentum, the movement spread swiftly to other cities and towns. In most locations the anarchist groups fell into three categories: Anarchist-Communists, Anarcho-Syndicalists and Individualist Anarchists. The Anarchist-Communists, drawing their inspiration from Bakunin and Kropotkin, envisioned a free federation of communities in which each member would be rewarded according to his needs (Document 17). Viewing the millennium in a romantic mirror which reflected a pre-industrial Russia of agricultural communes and handicrafts cooperatives, they had little use for large-scale industry or bureaucratic labour organizations. In the turmoil following the February Revolution they proceeded to confiscate a number of private residences – the most important were the Petrograd villa of P. P. Durnovo and the old Merchants' Club in Moscow (which was rechristened the House of Anarchy) – as headquarters for their egalitarian communes (Document 16).

The Anarcho-Syndicalists, on the other hand, pinned their hopes on the factory committees, which sprang up in the wake of the revolution, as the nuclei of the future libertarian society. The prospect of a new world centred around industrial production did not repel them in the least. Indeed, at times they exhibited an almost futuristic devotion to the cult of the machine. Theirs was the Westernizers' admiration of technological progress, in contrast to the Slavophile longing of the Anarchist-Communists for an irretrievable age that perhaps had never existed in the first place. Yet the Syndicalists did not yield to an uncritical worship of mass production.

[1] *Vol'nyi Kronshtadt*, 12 October 1917, p. 4.

The roots of Russian anarchism: right,
'Arise ye dead of the Paris Commune
under the red flag of the soviets'. The
events in Paris of 1871 represented
for many anarchists a consecrated ideal.
Below left, *Mikhail Aleksandrovich
Bakunin (1814–76), a founder of the
anarchist movement and a Promethean
figure who made his name a legend
throughout Europe;* right, his leading
disciple, *Peter Alekseevich Kropotkin
(1842–1921), came like Bakunin from
an aristocratic background but exerted a
milder, more intellectual and more
constructive influence on Russian
anarchism.*

Deeply influenced by Bakunin and Kropotkin, they anticipated the danger that man might be trapped in the gears and levers of a centralized industrial machine. They too looked backwards for a way out, to a decentralized society of labour organizations in which the workers could truly be masters of their own fate.

The immediate object of the Syndicalists was to introduce a broad measure of workers' control over production, which meant that the factory committees would take part in such matters as hiring and firing, establishing work rules and fixing wages, hours and conditions of labour (Documents 11 b, 12, 13). By the autumn of 1917 some form of workers' control had taken root in the vast majority of Russian factories, and there were even sporadic instances in which the factory committees expelled their employers, foremen and technical specialists and tried to run the enterprises themselves, sending delegations in search of fuel, raw materials and financial aid from the workers' committees in other establishments. Yet workers' control, at least in its more extreme forms, had a decidedly negative effect on production. For the workers were not only striving to maintain operations in the face of a wrecked transportation system and severe shortages of fuel and raw materials, but their inadequate technical and administrative knowledge could hardly fill the gap created by their expulsion of engineers and managers from the factories. In a revealing admission, the anarchist leader Emma Goldman noted that one large Petrograd factory remained in good working order during the Civil War only 'because the former owner and manager himself was still in charge'.[1]

Nevertheless, with their slogan of 'workers' control' the Syndicalists came to exert an influence in the labour movement quite out of proportion to their numbers. They were particularly influential among the bakers, miners, stevedores and postal workers, and played an important part in the All-Russian Conference of Factory Committees which met in Petrograd on the eve of the October Revolution. But because they repudiated a centralized party apparatus they were never in a position to lead the working class on a broad scale. In the end, it was left to the Bolsheviks, who were equipped not only with an effective party organization but also with the conscious will to power that the Syndicalists lacked, to capture the allegiance of the industrial workers in the factory committees and trade unions.

The Individualist Anarchists rejected both the territorial communes of the Anarchist-Communists and the workers' organizations of the Syndicalists. Only unorganized individuals, they believed, were safe from coercion and domination and thus capable of remaining true to the ideals of anarchism. Taking their cue from Nietzsche and Max Stirner, they

---

[1] Emma Goldman, *Living My Life* (2 vols., New York, 1931), II, 791.

Count Lev Nikolaevich Tolstoy (1828–1910) walking near his estate at Yasnaya Polyana. Although the Christian quietism of his followers was opposed to violent revolution, Tolstoy's castigation of authoritarianism, institutionalized religion, patriotism and war earned considerable respect and admiration from the Russian anarchists.

exalted the ego over and above the claims of collective entities and in some cases exhibited a distinctly aristocratic style of thought and action (Documents 8a, 8b). Anarcho-Individualism attracted a small following of Bohemian artists and intellectuals, and occasional lone-wolf bandits who found expression for their social alienation in violence and crime, with death as the ultimate form of self-affirmation, the ultimate escape from the constricting fabric of organized society. Here and there, by contrast, groups of Tolstoyans preached the gospel of Christian non-violence – it was said that they refused to kill even the lice which they plucked from their beards – and though they had few ties with the revolutionary anarchists, their moral impact on the movement was considerable.

While the anarchists did not attract a very large following, they had an influence in the Revolution and Civil War out of all proportion to their numbers. From the sketchy data available – the anarchists of course issued no 'party cards' and generally shunned formal organizational machinery – there appear to have been about ten thousand active anarchists in Russia at the height of the movement, not counting the Tolstoyans or Makhno's peasant movement in the Ukraine or the many thousands of sympathizers who regularly read anarchist literature and closely followed the movement's activities without taking a direct part in them.

ANARCHISTS AND BOLSHEVIKS

For all the anarchist groups the great hopes stirred by the February Revolution soon turned to bitter disappointment. The monarchy had been overthrown, and yet the state was left standing. What had taken place in February? asked an anarchist journal in Rostov-on-Don. 'Nothing special. In place of Nicholas the Bloody, Kerensky the Bloody has mounted the throne' (Document 21). The anarchists could not rest until the Provisional Government, like its tsarist predecessor, had been swept away. Before long, they found themselves making common cause with their ideological adversaries, the Bolsheviks, the only other radical group in Russia pressing for the immediate destruction of the 'bourgeois' state.

The intense hostility long felt by the anarchists towards Lenin dissipated rapidly as 1917 moved forward. Impressed by a series of ultra-radical statements Lenin had been making since his return to Russia, some anarchists came to believe that the Bolshevik leader had shed the straitjacket of Marxism for a new theory of revolution quite like their own (Document 20). Lenin's April Theses, for example, contained an array of iconoclastic propositions that anarchist thinkers had long cherished: the transformation of the 'predatory imperialist' war into a revolutionary struggle against the capitalist order; the renunciation of parliamentary government in favour of a regime of soviets patterned after the Paris Commune; the abolition of the police, the army and the bureaucracy; the

Vladimir Ilyich Lenin (Ulyanov) at the Third Congress of the Comintern in 1921, shortly after the suppression of the Kronstadt uprising.

levelling of incomes.[1] Although Lenin's preoccupation with the seizure of power gave pause to some, more than a few anarchists found his views sufficiently harmonious with their own to serve as a basis of cooperation. Whatever suspicions they still harboured were for the moment put aside. Lenin's appeal for 'a break-up and a revolution a thousand times more powerful than that of February'[2] had a distinctly Bakuninist ring and was precisely what most anarchists wanted to hear. Indeed, one anarchist leader in Petrograd was convinced that Lenin intended to inaugurate anarchism by 'withering away the state' the moment he got hold of it.[3]

Thus it happened that, during the eight months separating the two revolutions of 1917, both the anarchists and the Bolsheviks were bending their efforts towards the same goal, the destruction of the Provisional Government. Though a degree of wariness persisted on both sides, a prominent anarchist noted that on most vital questions there existed 'a perfect parallelism' between the two groups.[4] Their slogans – 'Down with the war! Down with the Provisional Government! Control of the factories to the workers! The land to the peasants!' – were often identical, and there even developed a certain *camaraderie* between the long-time antagonists engendered by their common purpose. When a Marxist lecturer told an audience of factory workers in Petrograd that the anarchists were disrupting the solidarity of Russian labour, an irate listener shouted, 'That's enough! The anarchists are our friends!' A second voice, however, was heard to mutter, 'God save us from such friends!'[5]

Although the anarchists and Bolsheviks were united in their determination to overthrow the Provisional Government, discord arose between them over the question of timing. During the spring and summer of 1917, Anarchist-Communist militants in the capital and at Kronstadt pressed for an immediate rising, while the Petrograd Bolshevik Committee argued that the moment was not yet ripe, that an undisciplined outburst by anarchists and rank-and-file Bolsheviks would be easily crushed, causing irreparable damage to the party and the revolution. The Anarchist-Communists, however, would have no truck with the temporizing of any political group, the Bolsheviks included. Impatient for the millennium, they pushed ahead with their plans for an armed insurrection. Anarchist agitators exhorted their listeners to revolt without further delay, assuring them that no assistance was needed from political organizations 'for the

---

[1] V.I. Lenin, *Polnoe sobranie sochinenii* (5th edn, 55 vols., Moscow, 1958–65), XXXI, 103–12.

[2] Ibid., XXXII, 441.

[3] Bertram D. Wolfe, Introduction to John Reed, *Ten Days That Shook the World* (New York, 1960), XXXI.

[4] Voline, *La Révolution inconnue (1917–1921)* (Paris, 1947), 185.

[5] *Novaia Zhizn*, 15 November 1917, p. 1.

February Revolution also took place without the leadership of a party'.[1]

The anarchists did not have long to wait. On 3 July crowds of soldiers, Kronstadt sailors and workmen erupted into open rebellion in the capital, demanding that the Petrograd Soviet assume power (though the anarchists among them were more interested in destroying the state than in transferring the reins of authority to the soviets). The Petrograd Soviet, however, refused to endorse the premature rising, and after a few days of sporadic disturbances the rioters were suppressed. It would be an exaggeration to call the July Days an 'anarchist creation', as did one speaker at an anarchist conference in 1918.[2] On the other hand, the role of the anarchists should not be minimized. Together with rank-and-file Bolsheviks and unaffiliated radicals, they acted as gadflies, goading the soldiers, sailors and workers into the abortive revolt.

THE OCTOBER REVOLUTION

In the wake of the July Days, the fears of the Bolshevik Committee were in part realized, as leaders of the party were arrested or forced into hiding. The Bolsheviks, however, were far from being crushed. Indeed, by October they were strong enough to launch their successful insurrection against the Kerensky regime, an insurrection in which the anarchists once again were among the most energetic participants. (There were at least four anarchist members of the Bolshevik-dominated Military Revolutionary Committee, which engineered the *coup d'état* of 25 October.) Disregarding the preachments of Bakunin and Kropotkin against political *coups*, the anarchists took part in the seizure of power in the belief that power, once captured, could somehow be diffused and eliminated.

Scarcely a day had passed, however, before they began to have second thoughts. On 26 October, when the Bolsheviks proclaimed a new 'Soviet government' and created a central Council of People's Commissars (Sovnarkom) composed exclusively of members of their own party, many anarchists recalled the warnings of Bakunin and Kropotkin that the 'dictatorship of the proletariat' would really mean 'the dictatorship of the Social Democratic party'.[3] At once they began to protest, arguing that such a concentration of political power would destroy the social revolution begun in February. The success of the revolution, they insisted, hinged on the decentralization of political and economic authority. The soviets and factory committees must remain decentralized units free from the domination of party bosses or so-called people's commissars. If any political group

---

[1] Leon Trotsky, *The History of the Russian Revolution* (3 vols. in 1, Ann Arbor, 1957), II, 82.

[2] *Burevestnik*, 11 April 1918, p. 2.

[3] *Svobodnaia Kommuna*, 2 October 1917, p. 2.

should attempt to convert them into instruments of coercion, the people must be ready to take up arms once more (Document 25).

Anarchist circles in Petrograd were soon buzzing with talk of a 'third and last stage of the revolution', a final struggle between 'authority and freedom . . . between two long contending social ideals: the Marxist and the anarchist' (Document 23). There were ominous murmurings among the Kronstadt sailors to the effect that, if the new Sovnarkom dared betray the revolution, the cannon that took the Winter Palace would take Smolny (headquarters of the Bolshevik government) as well. 'Where authority begins, there the revolution ends!'[1]

The grievances of the anarchists accumulated rapidly. On 2 November the new government published a Declaration of the Rights of the Peoples of Russia which affirmed the 'inalienable right' of every nationality to express its self-determination by establishing an independent state. For the anarchists this represented a step backward, a retreat from the internationalist and stateless ideal. By the spring of 1918 a new political police, the Cheka, had been established, the land had been nationalized, the factory committees had been subordinated to a state-controlled network of trade unions – in short, a 'commissarocracy' had been erected, 'the ulcer of our time', as the Kharkov Anarchist-Communist Association acridly described it.[2] According to an anonymous anarchist pamphlet of this period, the concentration of authority in the hands of the Sovnarkom, the Cheka and the Vesenkha (Supreme Economic Council) had cut short all hope for a free Russia: 'Bolshevism, day by day and step by step, proves that state power possesses inalienable characteristics; it can change its label, its "theory", and its servitors, but in essence it merely remains power and despotism in new forms.'[3]

The Paris Commune, once invoked as the ideal society to replace the Provisional Government, now became the anarchist answer to Lenin's dictatorship. The industrial workers were told to 'reject the words, orders and decrees of the commissars' and to create their own libertarian communes after the model of 1871.[4] At the same time, the anarchists had equal scorn for the 'parliamentary fetishism' of the Kadets, Socialist Revolutionaries and Mensheviks, and it is fitting that an anarchist sailor from Kronstadt, Anatoli Zhelezniakov, should have led the detachment which dispersed the Constituent Assembly in January 1918, ending its life of a single day (Documents 27, 28).

The stream of invective against the Soviet government reached a peak in February 1918, when the Bolsheviks resumed their peace negotiations

[1] *Golos Truda*, 4 November 1917, p. 1.
[2] *Bezvlastie*, March 1918, p. 1.
[3] *Velikii opyt* (n. p., 1918).
[4] *Burevestnik*, 9 April 1918, p. 2.

with the Germans at Brest-Litovsk. Anarchists joined with other 'internationalists' of the Left – Left SRs, Menshevik Internationalists, Left Communists – to protest against any accommodation with German 'imperialism'. To Lenin's contention that the Russian Army was too exhausted to fight any longer, the anarchists replied that professional armies were obsolete in any case, that the defence of the revolution was now the mission of the popular masses organized in partisan detachments. A leading Anarchist-Communist, Alexander Ge, spoke out vehemently against the conclusion of a peace treaty: 'The Anarchist-Communists proclaim terror and partisan warfare on two fronts. It is better to die for the world-wide socialist revolution than to live as the result of an agreement with German imperialism.'[1] The Anarchist-Communists and their Syndicalist comrades argued that bands of guerrilla fighters, organized spontaneously in local districts, would harass and demoralize the invaders, ultimately destroying them just as Napoleon's army had been destroyed in 1812. Volin, a prominent Syndicalist leader, sketched this strategy in vivid terms: 'The whole task is to hold on. To resist. Not to yield. To fight. To wage relentless partisan warfare – here and there and everywhere. To advance. Or falling back, to destroy. To torment, to harass, to prey upon the enemy' (Document 30).

But the appeals of the anarchists fell on deaf ears. The Brest-Litovsk treaty, even harsher than Ge and Volin had feared, was signed by the Bolshevik delegation on 3 March 1918. Lenin insisted that the agreement, severe as it was, provided a desperately needed breathing spell which would enable his party to consolidate the revolution and then carry it forward. For the outraged anarchists, however, the treaty was a humiliating capitulation to the forces of reaction, a betrayal of the world-wide revolution. It was indeed an 'obscene peace', they said, echoing Lenin's own description.[2] When the Fourth Congress of Soviets convened on 14 March to ratify the treaty, Alexander Ge and his fellow anarchist delegates (there were fourteen in all) voted in opposition.[3]

The dispute over the treaty of Brest-Litovsk threw into relief the growing estrangement between the anarchists and the Bolshevik party. With the overthrow of the Provisional Government in October 1917, their marriage of convenience had accomplished its purpose. By the spring of 1918 the majority of anarchists had become sufficiently disillusioned with Lenin to seek a complete break, while the Bolsheviks for their part had begun to contemplate the suppression of their former allies, who had outlived their usefulness and whose incessant criticisms were a nuisance the new regime need no longer tolerate. The anarchists, moreover, beyond their irritating

[1] *Pravda*, 25 February 1918, p. 2.
[2] *Bol'shevistskaia diktatura v svete anarkhizma* (Paris, 1928), 10.
[3] *Izvestiia VTsIK*, 17 March 1918, p. 2.

verbal assaults, were beginning to present a more tangible danger. Partly in preparation for the anticipated guerrilla war against Germany, and partly to discourage hostile manoeuvres by the Soviet government, local anarchist clubs had been organizing detachments of 'Black Guards' (the black flag was the anarchist emblem) armed with rifles, pistols and grenades.

An open break occurred in April 1918, when the Cheka launched a campaign to remove the more dangerous anarchist cells from Moscow and Petrograd. The most severe action took place on 11 April, when midnight raids were carried out against twenty-six anarchist centres in Moscow, during which forty anarchists were killed or wounded and more than five hundred arrested. In protest, the anarchists cried out that the Bolsheviks were a caste of self-seeking intellectuals who had betrayed the masses and the revolution (Document 33). Political power, they declared, always corrupts those who wield it and robs the people of their freedom. But if the golden age was slipping from their grasp, the anarchists refused to despair. They clung tenaciously to the belief that ultimately their vision of a stateless Utopia would triumph. 'Let us fight on,' they proclaimed, 'and our slogan shall be "The Revolution is dead! Long live the Revolution!"'[1]

THE CIVIL WAR

When the first shots of the Russian Civil War were fired, the anarchists, in common with the other left-wing opposition parties, were faced with a serious dilemma. Which side were they to support? As staunch libertarians, they held no brief for the dictatorial policies of Lenin's government. But the prospect of a White victory seemed even worse. Active opposition to the Soviet regime might tip the balance in favour of the counter-revolutionaries. On the other hand, support for the Bolsheviks might serve to entrench them too deeply to be ousted from power once the danger of reaction had passed. It was a quandary with no simple solution. After much soul-searching and debate, the anarchists adopted a variety of positions, ranging from active resistance to the Bolsheviks through passive neutrality to eager collaboration. A majority, however, cast in their lot with the beleaguered Soviet regime. By August 1919, at the climax of the Civil War, Lenin was so impressed with the zeal and courage of these 'Soviet anarchists', as their anti-Bolshevik comrades scornfully dubbed them, that he counted them among 'the most dedicated supports of Soviet power'.[2]

An outstanding case in point was Bill Shatov, a former IWW agitator in the United States who had returned to his native Russia after the February Revolution. As an officer in the Tenth Red Army during the autumn of 1919, Shatov threw his energies into the defence of Petrograd against the advance of General Yudenich. The following year he was summoned to

[1] G. P. Maksimov, *The Guillotine at Work* (Chicago, 1940), 23.
[2] Lenin, *Polnoe sobranie sochinenii*, XXXIX, 161.

Chita to become minister of transport in the Far Eastern Republic. Before he left, Shatov tried to justify his collaborationist position to his fellow libertarians, Emma Goldman and Alexander Berkman. 'Now I just want to tell you,' he said, 'that the Communist state in action is exactly what we anarchists have always claimed it would be – a tightly centralized power still more strengthened by the dangers of the Revolution. Under such conditions, one cannot do as one wills. One does not just hop on a train and go, or even ride the bumpers, as I used to do in the United States. One needs permission. But don't get the idea that I miss my American "blessings". Me for Russia, the Revolution, and its glorious future.' The anarchists, said Shatov, were 'the romanticists of the Revolution', but one could not fight with ideals alone. At the moment, the chief task was to defeat the re-actionaries. 'We anarchists should remain true to our ideals, but we should not criticize at this time. We must work and help to build' (Document 31).[1]

Shatov was one of a small army of anarchists who took up weapons against the Whites during the Civil War. Others accepted minor posts within the Soviet government and urged their comrades to do likewise, or at least to refrain from activities which were hostile to the Bolshevik cause. Iuda Roshchin, a former terrorist and an implacable foe of the Marxists, now surprised everyone by hailing Lenin as one of the great figures of the modern age. According to Victor Serge, Roshchin even tried to work out a 'libertarian theory of the dictatorship of the proletariat'.[2] Speaking before a group of Moscow anarchists in 1920, he exhorted his colleagues to co-operate with Lenin's party. 'It is the duty of every anarchist,' he declared, 'to work whole-heartedly with the Communists, who are the advance guard of the Revolution. Leave your theories alone, and do practical work for the reconstruction of Russia. The need is great, and the Bolsheviks welcome you' (Document 31).

But Roshchin's listeners were not impressed. Greeting his speech with a chorus of jeers and catcalls, they wrote him off as another loss to 'Soviet anarchism' and a traitor to the cause of Bakunin and Kropotkin. For even in these precarious circumstances a large and militant segment of the anarchist movement would deny their Bolshevik adversaries any quarter. The Briansk Federation of Anarchists, for example, called for the immediate overthrow of the 'Social Vampires' in the Kremlin who sucked the blood of the people (Document 34). Translating this appeal into action, a terrorist organization in Moscow known as the Underground Anarchists joined forces with the Left SRs and bombed the headquarters of the Communist Party Committee, killing twelve of its members and wounding fifty-five others, Bukharin among them.

In the south, where the authority of the state was completely disrupted,

[1] Cf. Alexander Berkman, *The Bolshevik Myth* (New York, 1925), 35–6.
[2] Victor Serge, *Memoirs of a Revolutionary, 1901–1941* (London, 1963), 120.

anarchist violence found its most fertile soil. Bands of armed marauders, operating under such names as 'Hurricane' and 'Death', sprang up in every quarter, ready to swoop down on town or village whenever the opportunity presented itself. The Bakunin Partisans of Ekaterinoslav sang of a new 'era of dynamite' which would greet oppressors of every persuasion, Red and White alike (Document 35). And in Kharkov a fanatical circle of Anarcho-Futurists proclaimed 'Death to world Civilization!' and urged the dark masses to take up their axes and destroy everything in sight (Document 7 c).

Anarchists of a more pacific bent denounced these groups as 'Sicilian bandits' who used the cloak of anarchism to conceal the predatory nature of their activities. For the moderates, robbery and terrorism were grotesque caricatures of anarchist doctrine which served only to demoralize the movement's true adherents and to discredit anarchism in the eyes of the public (Document 32). Renouncing violent action, the milder anarchists armed themselves with nothing more lethal than pen and ink and mounted a verbal attack on the Soviet dictatorship. A major theme of their criticism was that the Bolshevik Revolution had merely substituted 'state capitalism' for private capitalism, that one big owner had taken the place of many small ones, so that the peasants and workers now found themselves under the heel of a 'new class of administrators – a new class born mainly from the womb of the intelligentsia'. In their view, what had taken place in Russia closely resembled the earlier revolutions in Western Europe: no sooner had the oppressed farmers and craftsmen of England and France removed the landed aristocracy from power than the ambitious middle class stepped into the breach and erected a new class structure with itself at the top; in a similar manner, the privileges and authority once shared by the Russian nobility and *bourgeoisie* had passed into the hands of a new ruling class composed of party officials, government bureaucrats and technical specialists (Document 39).

As the Civil War deepened, the government grew less and less tolerant of such criticisms and started clamping down on anarchist groups in Moscow and Petrograd. Libertarian journals were closed, and clubs and organizations were forced to shut their doors or go underground. By way of justification, government spokesmen argued that the country was in a life-and-death struggle, beset by a staggering economic crisis and by powerful enemies on every side who longed to see the Bolsheviks ousted from power. Bolshevik Russia, they insisted, whatever its shortcomings, was the first socialist state in history, the first country in which the landlords and capitalists had been driven from their entrenched power. A White victory would mean a return to injustice and exploitation, and to the sterile and outmoded policies of the past; it would mean yet another dictatorship, but anti-proletarian rather than anti-bourgeois. The Bolsheviks were in no mood to tolerate threats from any group, especially a group which had militantly opposed the Brest-Litovsk treaty and organized Black Guard detachments which might stir up a good deal of trouble in the capital. For the fate of the revolution, as Trotsky put it, hung by a thread from day to day.

So the repressions continued. And as a result, there began an exodus of anarchists to the Ukraine, the perennial haven of fugitives from the persecutions of the central government. In the city of Kharkov a new anarchist organization, the *Nabat* (Alarm) Confederation, sprang up in 1918 and could soon boast flourishing branches in all the major cities of the south. As might be expected, *Nabat*'s adherents were extremely critical of the Soviet dictatorship, yet they believed that the most pressing task of the anarchist movement was to defend the revolution against the White onslaught, even if this should mean a temporary alliance with the Communists. To save the revolution they pinned their hopes on a 'partisan army' organized spontaneously by the revolutionary masses themselves (Document 40).

NESTOR MAKHNO

As the most likely nucleus of such an army the *Nabat* leaders looked to the guerrilla band led by Nestor Makhno, whose followers regarded him as a new Stenka Razin or Pugachev sent to realize their ancient dream of land and liberty. Travelling on horseback and in light peasant carts (*tachanki*) on which machine-guns were mounted, Makhno and his men moved swiftly back and forth across the open steppe between the Dnieper and the Sea of Azov, swelling into a small army as they went and inspiring terror in the hearts of their adversaries. Hitherto independent guerrilla bands accepted Makhno's command and rallied to his black banner. Villagers willingly provided food and fresh horses, enabling the Makhnovists to travel long distances with little difficulty. They would turn up suddenly where least expected, attack the gentry and military garrisons, then vanish as quickly as they had come. In captured uniforms they infiltrated the enemy's ranks to learn their plans or to fire on them at point-blank range. When cornered, the Makhnovists would bury their weapons, make their way singly back to their villages, and take up work in the fields, awaiting the next signal to unearth a new cache of arms and spring up again in an unexpected quarter. Makhno's insurgents, in the words of Victor Serge, revealed 'a truly epic capacity for organization and battle'.[1] Yet they owed much of their success to the exceptional qualities of their leader. Makhno was a bold and resourceful commander who combined an iron will with a quick sense of humour and won the love and devotion of his peasant followers. In September 1918, when he defeated a greatly

[1] Victor Serge, *op. cit.*

23

superior force of Austrians at the village of Dibrivki, his men honoured him with the affectionate title of *batko*, their 'dear father'.[1]

For a time Makhno's dealings with the Bolsheviks remained reasonably friendly, and the Soviet press extolled him as a 'courageous partisan' and a great revolutionary leader. Relations were at their best in March 1919, when Makhno and the Communists concluded a pact for joint military action against the White Army of General Denikin. Such gestures of harmony, however, could not conceal the basic hostility between the two groups. The Communists had little taste for the autonomous status of Makhno's Insurgent Army or for the powerful attraction which it exerted on their own peasant recruits; the Makhnovists, on their side, feared that sooner or later the Red Army would attempt to bring their movement to heel. As friction increased, the Soviet newspapers abandoned their eulogies of the Makhnovists and began to attack them as 'kulaks' and 'Anarcho-Bandits'. In May two Cheka agents sent to assassinate Makhno were caught and executed. The following month Trotsky, commander-in-chief of the Bolshevik forces, outlawed Makhno, and Communist troops carried out a lightning raid on his headquarters at Gulyai-Polye.

That summer, however, the shaky alliance was hastily resumed when Denikin's massive drive towards Moscow sent both the Communists and the Makhnovists reeling. On 26 September 1919, Makhno suddenly launched a successful counter-attack at the village of Peregonovka, near the town of Uman, cutting the White general's supply lines and creating panic and disorder in his rear. This was Denikin's first serious reverse in his dramatic advance into the Russian heartland and a major factor in halting his drive towards the Bolshevik capital. By the end of the year a counter-offensive by the Red Army had forced Denikin to beat a swift retreat to the shores of the Black Sea.

The *Makhnovshchina* reached its peak in the months following the victory at Peregonovka. During October and November Makhno occupied Ekaterinoslav and Aleksandrovsk for several weeks and thus obtained his first chance to apply the concepts of anarchism to city life, something he had already attempted in the countryside with the formation of libertarian communes (Documents 41, 42). Makhno's aim was to throw off domination of every type and to encourage economic and social self-determination. For example, when the railway workers of Aleksandrovsk complained that they had not been paid for many weeks, he advised them to take control of the railway lines and charge the passengers and freight shippers what seemed a fair price for their services. Such Utopian projects, however, failed to win over more than a small minority of working men, for, unlike the farmers and artisans of the village, who were independent

[1] P. A. Arshinov, *Istoriia makhnovskogo dvizheniia (1918–1921 gg.)* (Berlin, 1923), 57–8.

producers accustomed to managing their own affairs, factory workers and miners operated as interdependent parts of a complicated industrial machine and were lost without the guidance of supervisors and technical specialists. Furthermore, the peasants and artisans could barter the products of their labour, whereas the urban workers depended on regular wages for their survival. Makhno, moreover, compounded the confusion when he recognized all paper money issued by his predecessors – Ukrainian nationalists, Whites and Bolsheviks alike. He never understood the complexities of an urban economy, nor did he care to understand them. He detested the 'poison' of the cities and cherished the natural simplicity of the peasant environment into which he had been born (Documents 43, 44, 45). In any event, Makhno found very little time to implement his ill-defined economic programmes. He was forever on the move, rarely pausing to catch his breath. The *Makhnovshchina*, in the words of one of the *batko*'s associates, was a 'republic on *tachanki*. . . . As always, the instability of the situation prevented positive work.'[1]

At the end of 1919 Makhno received instructions from the Red Command to transfer his army to the Polish front. The order was plainly designed to draw the Makhnovists away from their home territory and thus leave it open to the establishment of Bolshevik rule. Makhno refused to budge. Trotsky's response was firm and unhesitating: he outlawed the Makhnovists and sent his troops against them. There ensued eight months of bitter struggle with losses high on both sides. A severe typhus epidemic augmented the toll of victims. Badly outnumbered, Makhno's partisans avoided pitched battles and relied on the guerrilla tactics they had perfected in more than two years of civil war.

Hostilities were broken off in October 1920, when Baron Wrangel, Denikin's successor in the south, launched a major offensive, striking northward from the Crimean peninsula. Once more the Red Army enlisted Makhno's aid, in return for which the Communists agreed to amnesty all anarchists in Russian prisons and guaranteed the anarchists freedom of propaganda on condition that they refrain from calling for the violent overthrow of the Soviet government. Barely a month later, however, the Red Army had made sufficient gains to assure victory in the Civil War, and the Soviet leaders tore up their agreement with Makhno. Not only had the Makhnovists outlived their usefulness as military partners, but as long as the *batko* was left at large the spirit of primitive anarchism and the danger of a peasant *jacquerie* would remain to haunt the unsteady Bolshevik regime. Thus, on 25 November 1920, Makhno's commanders in the Crimea, fresh from their victories over Wrangel's army, were seized by the Red Army and immediately shot. The next day Trotsky ordered an attack on Makhno's headquarters in Gulyai-Polye, while the Cheka simultaneously arrested

[1] Voline, *La Révolution inconnue*, 578, 603.

the members of the *Nabat* Confederation in Kharkov and carried out raids on anarchist clubs and organizations throughout the country. During the attack on Gulyai-Polye, most of Makhno's staff were captured and imprisoned or simply shot on the spot. The *batko* himself, however, together with a battered remnant of an army which had once numbered tens of thousands, managed to elude his pursuers. After wandering over the Ukraine for the better part of a year, the partisan leader, exhausted and still suffering from unhealed wounds, crossed the Dniester River into Rumania and eventually found his way to Paris.

REPRESSION

The downfall of Makhno marked the beginning of the end of Russian anarchism. Three months later, in February 1921, the movement suffered another major blow when Peter Kropotkin, nearly eighty years old, fell ill with pneumonia and died (Documents 48, 49). Kropotkin's family declined Lenin's offer of a state burial, and a committee of anarchists was set up to arrange a funeral. Lev Kamenev, chairman of the Moscow Soviet, allowed a handful of imprisoned anarchists a day's liberty to take part in the procession. Braving the bitter cold of the Moscow winter, tens of thousands marched in the cortège to the Novodevichi Monastery, the burial place of Kropotkin's princely ancestors. They carried placards and black banners bearing demands for the release of all anarchists from prison and such mottoes as 'Where there is authority there is no freedom' and 'The liberation of the working class is the task of the workers themselves'. A chorus chanted 'Eternal Memory'. As the procession passed the Butyrki prison, the inmates shook the bars on their windows and sang an anarchist hymn to the dead. Emma Goldman spoke at Kropotkin's graveside, and students and workers placed flowers by his tomb. Kropotkin's birthplace, a large house in the old aristocratic quarter of Moscow, was turned over to his wife and comrades to be used as a museum for his books, papers and personal belongings. Supervised by a committee of scholarly anarchists, it was maintained by contributions from friends and admirers throughout the world.[1]

At Kropotkin's funeral the black flag of anarchism was paraded through Moscow for the last time. Two weeks later the Kronstadt rebellion broke out, and a new wave of political arrests swept the country (Documents 50, 51, 52). Anarchist book stores, printing offices and clubs were closed and the few remaining anarchist circles broken up. Even the pacifist followers

---

[1] The museum was closed after the death of Kropotkin's widow in 1938. In 1967 the author visited the house and found it being used for a purpose of which Kropotkin himself would surely have approved: it serves as a school for British and American embassy children, with a playground in the garden and an interior filled with children's books and art work.

of Tolstoy – a number of whom had been shot during the Civil War for refusing to serve in the Red Army – were imprisoned or banished. In Moscow a circle of leading 'Soviet anarchists' known as the Universalists were arrested on trumped-up charges of 'banditry and underground activities', and their organization was replaced by a new group called the 'Anarcho-Biocosmists', who pledged unwavering support of the Soviet government and solemnly declared their intention to launch a social revolution 'in interplanetary space but not upon Soviet territory'.[1]

Repression continued unabated as the months advanced. In September 1921 the Cheka executed two well-known anarchists – Fanya Baron and Lev Cherny, the poet – without a trial and without bringing formal charges against them. Emma Goldman was so outraged that she considered making a scene in the manner of the English suffragettes by chaining herself to a bench in the hall where the Third Comintern Congress was meeting and shouting her protests to the delegates. She was dissuaded from doing so by her Russian friends, but soon afterwards she and Alexander Berkman, profoundly disheartened by the turn the revolution had taken, made up their minds to leave the country. 'Grey are the passing days,' Berkman recorded in his diary. 'One by one the embers of hope have died out. Terror and despotism have crushed the life born in October. The slogans of the Revolution are forsworn, its ideals stifled in the blood of the people. The breath of yesterday is dooming millions to death; the shadow of today hangs like a black pall over the country. Dictatorship is trampling the masses under foot. The Revolution is dead; its spirit cries in the wilderness. . . . I have decided to leave Russia' (Document 53).

CONCLUSION

Fifty years have passed since the suppression of the Russian anarchists, and, seen in historical perspective, their role in the Revolution of 1917 seems more impressive than ever. When reading the anarchist writings of the revolutionary period, one is struck again and again by how perceptive were their criticisms of authoritarian socialism, how prophetic their warnings of the dangers of centralized power, and how relevant their ideas for the present. With their vision of a decentralized society and their programme of direct action, the anarchists have exerted a lasting influence. In their criticisms of the 'new class', their passionate anti-militarism, their call for women's liberation, their inauguration of 'free universities', and their ecological concern for a balance between town and country, between Man and Nature, not to speak of their terrorist bombings and defiant courtroom behaviour, they sound astonishingly up to date. All this, indeed, goes a long way to explain the resurgence of interest in anarchism, particularly among the young, in recent years.

[1] Maksimov, *The Guillotine at Work*, 362.

The vitality of the anarchist vision has never been more apparent than at present. For a growing number of youthful rebels, libertarian socialism has become an alternative to bankrupt authoritarian socialism, especially as it has evolved in the Soviet Union under Communist rule. The dream of a decentralized society of autonomous communes and labour federations appeals more and more to those who are seeking to escape from a centralized, conformist and artificial world. It is small wonder, then, that the black banner has occasionally been unfurled in campus demonstrations from Berkeley to Paris. The emphasis which anarchists have laid on the natural, the spontaneous and the unsystematic, their urge towards a simpler and more equitable way of life, their distrust of bureaucracy and centralized authority, and their belief that social emancipation must be attained by libertarian rather than authoritarian means – all these hark back to the experience of the anarchists in the Russian Revolution. For socialism without liberty, as both Proudhon and Bakunin observed, is the worst form of tyranny. This, perhaps, has been the Revolution's most important lesson.

NOTE ON DOCUMENTS

During the Russian Revolution and Civil War the anarchist message was spread through pamphlets, newspapers, journals, leaflets, speeches, songs and poems. It is from such sources that the documents in this anthology have been drawn. In every case, rather than rely on secondary works, I have let the anarchists speak for themselves. Moreover, I have tried to avoid extracting bits and pieces from their speeches and writings. Wherever possible the complete document, or at least a substantial excerpt, is provided.

Nearly all the selections are here translated into English for the first time. In only a few cases were they originally written in English or were adequate translations already available. The style of the documents varies widely, being sometimes elegant, sometimes quite primitive. In my translations I have tried to preserve the flavour of the originals rather than to improve their literary quality, though on a few occasions I have smoothed out rough spots for the sake of clarity. Moreover, the extensive use of dots or italics or bold type for dramatic effect, and the practice of beginning new paragraphs with every second or third sentence, have been abandoned for the sake of readability or for considerations of space, except where they seem essential to preserve the tone of the original.

Finally, a word about dates and transliteration. The Western calendar was adopted by Soviet Russia in February 1918. Earlier dates are given in the old style, that is, according to the Julian calendar, which lagged thirteen days behind the Western calendar in the twentieth century. In transliterating Russian words and proper names, I have followed the Library of Congress system but in a slightly modified form for the sake of readability.

Soldiers and sailors listening to a speech by Mikhail Rodzianko in the Tauride (Tavrichesky) Palace, March 1917.

Part One
The February Revolution

The outbreak of the February Revolution, a spontaneous affair neither organized nor directed by any political group, found most of the leading Russian anarchists in foreign exile. Not surprisingly, when news of the rising reached them, they responded with great enthusiasm, tempered only by their frustration at being marooned in the West while their homeland was in the throes of revolution.

These emotions – enthusiasm and frustration – dominate the essays by Volin and Roshchin which form the opening selections of this anthology. At the time of the uprising Volin (the pseudonym of Vsevolod Mikhailovich Eikhenbaum) was in New York, having been expelled from France in 1916 for conducting anti-militarist propaganda. Roshchin (real name Iuda Solomonovich Grossman) was living in Geneva and, like Volin, was a prominent anarchist and a staunch opponent of the war. Both men longed to return to Russia and to take part in the rapidly unfolding events there. They finally succeeded in doing so during the summer of 1917. Volin became editor of the foremost Syndicalist journal Golos Truda (The Voice of Labour) and a prolific writer and lecturer. Roshchin, unlike his comrade, supported the Bolsheviks after the October Revolution and became a leading 'Soviet Anarchist' (see Document 31).

1 The Revolution Ahead   VOLIN

We are condemned to remain remote from events. We are unable for the moment to return there – to Russia, to the people in revolt, to our brothers, our comrades. We are separated from our homeland by land and sea, by earth and ocean. We have been torn from her by war.

From the venal, fraudulent newspapers here we obtain only pitiful fragments of the truth. Meanwhile, we are condemned to inaction. We are not the living participants of events. We are not even eyewitnesses. We are only distant, distant watchers. We cannot judge, decide, appeal. We can scarcely dare even to think.

But there is one thing that we can do. We have the right to say – indeed we must say – that what has so far taken place in Russia is not yet a revolution. Rodzianko is the 'leader' of this 'revolution'. The Duma is the centre. The army is the boss. The Lvovs and Miliukovs are the managers and directors. Property remains inviolate, war sacred.

And what is this 'song and dance' to the people – the tortured, starving, dying people, the peasants and workers? The peasants need the land – all

The Revolution of February 1917 in Nikolaevsk on the mouth of the Amur.
The banner reads: 'Long Live the People. Land Liberty Peace.'

Left, *Volin (Vsevolod Mikhailovich Eikhenbaum) in Paris after his deportation from Russia in January 1922 and* (right) *Mikhail Vladimirovich Rodzianko, one of the chief architects of the Provisional Government.*

the land. The workers need the mines, factories, shops, machines – all the means of production. The people need peace. The people need bread, homes, clothing. The people need freedom – full freedom to act.

Will they obtain all these necessities from the Rodziankos, the Lvovs, the Miliukovs,[1] or from any government or any authority whatever? Never. They must take everything themselves. Will they take it? Will events continue to broaden and deepen? Will this become a real popular cause? Here is the whole question.

If matters remain where they stand now, that is at the victory of the 'Russian Party' and at the establishment of a 'constitutional monarchist form of government' with ministers from the Kadet party, then you may call the episode what you will – a 'statist upheaval', a 'Kadet upheaval', a 'patriotic upheaval', or simply an 'upheaval' – only not a revolution. From such a 'revolution' the people, the peasants and workers, will not obtain a broken copeck.

But if events do not get stuck at a mere 'constitution'; if they stir up the popular masses and throw overboard once and for all the Nikolai Nikolaeviches,[2] Rodziankos, Miliukovs, Lvovs, and all other 'leaders', tsars and

---

[1] Rodzianko, Lvov, and Miliukov were principal figures in the transfer of power from the defunct autocracy to the Provisional Government. M. V. Rodzianko (1859–1924), an adherent of the conservative Octobrist party, was a member of the Duma committee which helped set up the Provisional Government in February 1917. Prince G. E. Lvov (1861–1925), a Constitutional Democrat (Kadet), was prime minister of the Provisional Government, and P. N. Miliukov (1859–1943), a well-known historian and leader of the Kadets, was his minister for foreign affairs.

[2] Grand Duke Nikolai Nikolaevich was an uncle of Tsar Nicholas II and commander-in-chief of the Russian Army during the first year of the war. Volin, however, probably means the tsar himself, Nikolai Aleksandrovich.

rulers; if the people take their fate in their own hands and everywhere proclaim 'free cities' and 'free villages', organize their peasants' and workers' unions, and begin to seize the land and the means of production, transportation and communication as common property; if the people themselves settle the question of war and peace – then and only then may we speak of a revolution. Only then will the heavy curtain rise which conceals the future destiny of Russia, of the other countries, and of the war itself.

Is there a chance that events will not remain in a blind alley but rather emerge on the broad path of revolution? Yes, there is. And we shall say something about this another time. Meanwhile, we will wait, hope, believe. At the present moment we are unable to act, decide, appeal. We are not the participants of events. We can only think, worry, desire. And our desire is clear: Down with government! Long live the revolution!

Volin, 'Revoliutsiia vperedi', *Revoliutsiia i anarkhizm*
(Kharkov, 1919), 11–12, reprinted from *Golos Truda* (New
York), 23 March 1917.

2 *A Greeting to Freedom* IUDA ROSHCHIN

> I have come to you with greetings,
> To tell you that the sun has risen. . . .

The sun has risen. It has dispersed the black clouds. The Russian people have awakened! Greetings to revolutionary Russia! Greetings to the fighters for the happiness of the people!

The grey autumnal days have passed. What gloom once enveloped us! How many mortal wounds it inflicted, the cursed past! How much strength was wasted for nothing. One of the greatest crimes of the old regime, perhaps, was that it sowed mistrust in the powers of Russia!

'Can the broad masses really live without happiness and freedom?' P. L. Lavrov once wrote.[1] We waited for a long time for this breakthrough to freedom, accomplished at last by those who were able to help awaken the slumbering giant. Years had gone by. Around us things grew blacker. The darkness grew more impenetrable, oppression more unbearable, compulsion more malevolent. And the failure of the 1905 Revolution sowed doubts in many souls. Perhaps Russia is ill. Perhaps he was right who said that 'the great sin of Russia is that it created a great literature without a great history'. But the March Days showed that Russia, following the example of other nations, is able to create a great history!

[1] Peter Lavrovich Lavrov (1823–1900), a leading Populist thinker whose writings had a great influence on the Russian revolutionary movement.

Greetings to revolutionary Russia! Greetings to the fighters for the happiness of the people! We now desire the expansion of the revolution, for we are convinced that only in a time of revolution will there awaken all the mighty and good forces that slumber in the soul of the people. Yet tired people tell us: 'Beware of the counter-revolution! Don't ask the impossible. Don't prepare with your own intransigence the soil for the triumph of reaction.' But is preserving what has already been won really intransigence? Is not the expansion of demands which flow from the depths of the people in fact the best means to combat the possibility of counter-revolution?

Tired people say: 'Be satisfied with the necessities. Don't demand luxuries.' We answer these tired people with the words of King Lear: 'The art of our necessities is strange, that can make vile things precious.' Look – the experience of the March Days has already refuted your imaginary realism. In good conscience you regarded reforms as urgent, you dreamed of a responsible ministry. Yet under the pressure of the popular masses what has been achieved is nothing less than the abdication of the tsar and the introduction of broad political freedom. What once seemed a 'luxury' at once became a necessity.

'A republic in Russia? Oh, that's madness, fantasy, the delirium of sick minds!' Yet now, under pressure from the masses, even the Kadets have inserted in their programme a point about a republic! No, gentlemen, he is no realist who regards freedom as a fragile vase that must be protected from sudden jolts. The realist is one who can inject into the social revolution the greatest number of ideas about freedom and can make these ideas not a luxury but a necessity for the masses.

Tell the people, then, that the free man needs no chains of law and authority. If you say this and awaken the spirit of freedom in the people, then historical necessity will be with you. . . . We shall unleash at this time all our slogans about bread and liberty and do all we can to avoid becoming a mere speck on the crest of the wave. We shall be neither inanimate puppets in the hands of events nor slaves of external necessity but shall deliver the people's ultimatum to the whole system of economic exploitation and statist enslavement.

We shall found a workers' organization capable of expressing this lofty idea as well as the will of free labour.

Greetings to revolutionary Russia!

Greetings to the fighters for the happiness of the people!

Roshchin, 'Privet svobode', *Put' k Svobode* (Geneva), May 1917, pp. 1–2, slightly abridged.

In the wake of the February Revolution, anarchist groups sprang up all over the country. A major libertarian stronghold throughout the revolution and Civil War was the Kronstadt naval station near Petrograd, the main base of the Baltic Fleet. Documents 3 and 4, which appeared in the anarchist journal Vol'nyi Kronshtadt *(Free Kronstadt), are brief but eloquent credos – one in prose, one in poetry – by rank-and-file Kronstadt anarchists.*

3 Why I Am an Anarchist   *N. PETROV*

I am an anarchist because contemporary society is divided into two opposing classes: the impoverished and dispossessed workers and peasants who have created with their own hands and their own enormous toil all the riches of the earth, and the rich men, kings and presidents who have confiscated all these riches for themselves. Towards these parasitic capitalists and ruling kings and presidents there arose in me a feeling of outrage, indignation, and loathing, while at the same time I felt sorrow and compassion for the labouring proletariat who have been eternal slaves in the vice-like grip of the world-wide *bourgeoisie*.

I am an anarchist because I scorn and detest all authority, since all authority is founded on injustice, exploitation and compulsion over the human personality. Authority dehumanizes the individual and makes him a slave.

I am an opponent of private property when it is held by individual capitalist parasites, for private property is theft.[1]

I am an anarchist because I subject to unstinting criticism and censure bourgeois morality as well as false and distorted bourgeois science and religion, which shroud the human personality in darkness and prevent its independent development.

I am an anarchist because I cannot remain silent while the propertied class oppresses and humiliates the propertyless toilers, the workers and peasants. In such circumstances only corpses can remain silent, not live human beings.

I am an anarchist because I believe in the truth of the anarchist ideal, which seeks to liberate mankind from the authority of capitalism and the deception of religion.

I am an anarchist because I believe only in the creative powers and independence of a united proletariat and not of the leaders of political parties of various kinds.

I am an anarchist because I believe that the present struggle between the classes will end only when the toiling masses, organized as a class, gain their true interests and conquer, by means of a violent social revolution, all

[1] The allusion here is to the famous dictum of Pierre-Joseph Proudhon, 'Property is theft'. A leading French radical, Proudhon (1809–65) was the first major figure to call himself an 'anarchist', and became one of the founding fathers of the anarchist movement.

the riches of the earth. Having accomplished such an overthrow and having abolished all institutions of government and authority, the oppressed class must proclaim a society of free producers which will endeavour to satisfy the needs of each individual, who must in turn give society his labour and his concern for the welfare of all mankind.

I am not deluded by the loud and vulgar 'socialist' phrase, 'dictatorship of the proletariat and peasantry'. Dictatorship is a synonym for authority, and authority is something alien to the masses. Authority always and everywhere corrupts the rulers, who play the role of flies on the horns of an ox in pasture, poisonous flies which from time to time bite the ox and contaminate its blood, draining its energy and killing its independent initiative.

I firmly believe that authority will disappear with the disappearance of capitalism. The popular masses themselves will conduct their affairs on equal and communal lines in free communities.

I am an anarchist because I strive by my own personal initiative to impress upon the masses the idea of anarchist communism. I interpret communism in the full sense of the word, for I shall find my own happiness in the common happiness of free and autonomous men like myself.

N. Petrov, 'Pochemu ia anarkhist', *Vol'nyi Kronshtadt*, 23 October 1917, pp. 2–3.

4 Appeal   SEAMAN STEPAN STEPANOV

> Come gather beneath the black banner
> Men of honour, of struggle and toil,
> Come ignite the fires of rebellion
> In the hearts of the chained and oppressed.
>
> Awaken your slumbering Russia
> Call the people to enter the fight
> To strike down the sated bloodsuckers
> And cast off the tyrannous yoke.
>
> Go down into the damp cellars
> Where the slaves of poverty die
> Where echo the moans of the injured
> And darkness reigns unopposed.
>
> Go down if your hearts are atremble
> If your spirits with goodness are full
> Where blood flows like rivers in springtime
> And the earth shakes from groans of the poor.

We are tired of this evil tragedy
Of the eternal torments of fate
So advance to the world of Anarchism
To the world of the sacred Commune.

Matros Stepan Stepanov, 'Prizyv', *Vol'nyi Kronshtadt*, 23
October 1917, p. 3.

*Poster of 1919 honouring the Red Fleet as the 'Vanguard
of the Revolution'. The unquestioned loyalty of the Russian
sailors to the Revolution in its early days made the
subsequent Kronstadt uprising (see pp. 156–65) a
particularly bitter blow for the Bolshevik leaders.*

Part Two
Aspects of Anarchism

Though all anarchists have been united in their opposition to coercion and exploitation, they have held a wide variety of views on many important subjects, ranging from religion and war to education and the nature of the future society. The documents in Part Two illustrate the richness of libertarian thought during the Russian Revolution and Civil War.

5 ATHEISM

In their ardent pursuit of the millennium the Russian anarchists exhibited some of the features of a religious movement. In many ways, indeed, they resembled such Christian sectarians as the Tolstoyans and the Dukhobors, who rejected compulsion and violence, refused to take oaths or bear arms, spurned the official church, and put their faith in a personal communion with Christ, whose kingdom, they said, reposed in the hearts of the faithful. At the same time, however, nearly all anarchist militants have been staunch atheists, unyielding in their opposition to God as well as to the state – 'my two bêtes noires', Bakunin once called them. Both secular and religious authority are equally repugnant to the libertarian spirit, and 'Neither God nor Master' is an effective summary of the anarchist message. 'The church has always been allied with the state in the subjugation of mankind', wrote Bakunin in God and the State, *the bible of anarchist atheism. Governments throughout history have used religion both as a means of keeping men in ignorance and as a safety-valve for human misery and frustration. Thus 'if God really existed,' Bakunin concluded, inverting a famous dictum of Voltaire's, 'it would be necessary to abolish him.' His disciples took up this message, as the following documents show, insisting that men will be free only when they have thrown off the double yoke of spiritual and temporal authority.*

5a Arise! *I. SELITSKY*

Arise! Arise people! Proclaim your mighty word: Enough! I do not wish to be an automaton. Away with all despots and parasites. I am a man! I want to live, to create my own life. I have the right to life and happiness. I want my happiness to be the happiness of others as well. I want my destiny to be no longer a plaything in the hands of despotic Gods of heaven or earth. At this moment, at this hour, I take my fate in my own hands and reject any further appeal to visible or invisible Gods.

'Civilization', a dramatic cartoon from Golos Truda (Petrograd, 20 October 1917) drawn by the American anarchist cartoonist Robert Minor, who later went over to the Communists.

You, Invisible Gods of the Heavens! You call yourselves Gods of justice. But where is your justice? You call yourselves Gods of truth. But where is your truth? You say you are punishing evil. But where is your punishment? You are omnipotent. But where is your power? You are ubiquitous. But where are you then? You are all-knowing Gods – you knew and permitted these crimes. And now that human beings perish by the thousands and the whole earth wallows in blood, you all-powerful Gods are powerless to stop this nightmarish drama of humanity. You are ubiquitous – looking in silence at the sea of tears and the rivers of blood. You have not a drop of compassion for the human beings you have created. You bless this orgy of animal passions. You thrive on blood. You thrive on death. You thrive on humanity's misfortune.

Thus you are the Gods not of life but of death, not of happiness but of misery, not of freedom but of oppression. You are all of you despots, criminals, tyrants. Bloodthirsty Gods. Your godly machinations are revealed in the following stupid desires: I want – I shall create. I want – I shall take. I want – for myself. I want – so he will remain in a fog.

Arise! Arise then people! Disperse the nightmare surrounding you. Take the voice of truth as your own possession. Put an end to all the stupid desires of earthly and heavenly deities. Say 'Enough – I have risen!'

And you will be free.

I. Selitskii, 'Prosnis'!', *Vol'nyi Kronshtadt*, 12 October 1917, p. 2, abridged. Written 19 September 1917.

5b Atheist Manifesto

It is hard to say when human thought first conceived of the existence of God. But once having conceived of him, it proceeded to reject him. Possibly the rejection of God occurred immediately after the first conception of him, the first recognition of his existence. In any event, the rejection of God is very old, and the seeds of unbelief appeared very early in the history of mankind. In the course of several centuries, however, these modest seeds of atheism were strangled by the poisonous nettles of theism. But the striving of human thought and feeling for freedom is too great not to prevail. And it has indeed prevailed. Beneath its pressures all religions have broadened their horizons, yielding one point after another and casting off much that only a generation ago was deemed indispensable. Religion, striving to preserve its existence, has made various compromises, piling one absurdity upon another, combining the uncombinable.

The naïve legends concerning the origins of the earth, legends created by pastoral folk at the dawn of life, were cast off and relegated to the mythology of 'holy books'. Beneath the pressure of science, religion repudiated the

Devil and repudiated the personification of the deity. Instead, God now reveals himself to us as Reason, Justice, Love, Mercy, etc., etc. Since it was impossible to salvage the contents of religion, men preserved its forms, knowing full well that the forms would give shape to whatever contents were placed in them.

The whole so-called progress of religion is nothing but a series of concessions to emancipated will, thought and feeling. Without their persistent attacks, religion would to this day preserve its original crude and naïve character. Thought, moreover, achieved other triumphs as well. Not only did it compel religion to become more progressive, or, more accurately, to give birth to new forms, but it also took an independent creative step, moving ever more boldly towards open, militant atheism.

And our atheism is militant atheism. We believe it is time to begin an open, ruthless struggle with all religious dogmas, whatever they may be called, whatever philosophical or moral systems may conceal their religious essence. We shall fight against all attempts to reform religion or to smuggle the outmoded concepts of past ages into the spiritual baggage of contemporary humanity. We find all gods equally repulsive, whether bloodthirsty or humane, envious or kind, vengeful or forgiving. What is important is not what sort of gods they are but simply that they are gods – that is, our lords, our sovereigns – and that we love our spiritual freedom too dearly to bow before them.

Therefore we are atheists. We shall boldly carry our propaganda of atheism to the toiling masses, for whom atheism is more necessary than anyone else. We fear not the reproach that by destroying the people's faith we are pulling the moral foundation from under their feet, a reproach uttered by 'lovers of the people' who maintain that religion and morality are inseparable. We assert, rather, that morality can and must be free from any ties with religion, basing our conviction on the teachings of contemporary science about morality and society. Only by destroying the old religious dogmas can we accomplish the great positive task of liberating thought and feeling from their old and rusty fetters. And what can better break such bonds?

We hold that there are no objective ideas either in the existing universe or in the past history of peoples. An objective world is nonsense. Desires and aspirations belong only to the individual personality, and we place the free individual in the main corner. We shall destroy the old, repulsive morality of religion which declares: 'Do good or God will punish you.' We oppose this bargaining and say: 'Do what you think is good without making deals with anyone but only because it is good.' Is this really only destructive work?

So much do we love the human personality that we must therefore hate gods. And therefore we are atheists. The age-old and difficult struggle of 41 the workers for the liberation of labour may continue even longer. The workers may have to toil even more than they already have, and to sacrifice their blood in order to consolidate what has already been won. Along the way, the workers will doubtless experience further defeats and, even worse, disillusionment. For this very reason they must have an iron heart and a mighty spirit which can withstand the blows of fate. But can a slave really have an iron heart? Under God all men are slaves and nonentities. And can men possess a mighty spirit when they fall on their knees and prostrate themselves, as do the faithful?

We shall therefore go to the workers and try to destroy the vestiges of their faith in God. We shall teach them to stand proud and upright as befits free men. We shall teach them to seek help only from themselves, in their own spirit and in the strength of free organizations. We are slandered with the charge that all our best feelings, thoughts, desires and acts are not our own, are not experienced by us, but are God's, are determined by God, and that we are not ourselves but a mere vehicle carrying out the will of God or the Devil. We want to take responsibility for everything upon ourselves. We want to be free. We do not want to be marionettes or puppets. Therefore we are atheists.

Religions recognize their inability to sustain man's belief in the Devil, and are rejecting that already discredited figure. But this is inconsistent, for the Devil has as much claim to existence as God – that is, none at all. Belief in the Devil was once very strong. There was a time when demonism held exclusive sway over men's minds, yet now this menacing figure and tempter of humanity has been transformed into a petty demon, more comical than frightening. The same fate must likewise befall his blood-brother – God.

God, the Devil, faith – mankind has paid for these awful words with a sea of blood, a river of tears, and endless suffering. Enough of this nightmare! Man must finally throw off the yoke, must become free. Sooner or later labour will win. But man must enter the society of equality, brotherhood and freedom ready and spiritually free, or at least free of the divine rubbish which has clung to him for a thousand years. We have shaken this poisonous dust from our feet, and we are therefore atheists.

Come with us all who love man and freedom and hate gods and slavery. Yes, the gods are dying! Long live man!

Union of Atheists

Soiuz Ateistov, 'Ateisticheskii manifest', *Nabat* (Kharkov),
12 May 1919, p. 3.

5c My God   *E. ZAIDNER-SADD*

I do not bow before that idol
To whom the wretched of the earth,
The world's enslaved, downtrodden children,
Convey their gifts and beg rewards.

Such a God gives me no comfort
Who pits the strong against the weak,
Who burdens men with trial and hardship
And makes of suffering a cult.

The gaze of his forbidding visage,
The pallor of his mournful brow
Ignite no fires within my bosom,
Nor warm my spirits late at night.

My God is an idea: a new life,
The dawn of bright and happy days,
To struggle, to ferocious struggle,
It summons all courageous men!

It brings revenge on the oppressors
Who deal with men by shedding blood!
My God is great and glorious freedom,
Self-awareness, strength, and love!

E. Zaidner-Sadd, 'Moi bog', *Ekaterinoslavskii Nabat*, 7
January 1920, p. 3.

*Russian regimental banner of the First World War with the motto, 'God Is
With Us'. The anarchists saw in the Church a bitter enemy, trading on the
simple piety of the ordinary people to buttress the oppressive machinery of state
and the armed forces.*

6 ANTI-MILITARISM

The anarchist movement has had a long tradition of resistance to war. Yet there have been occasions when leading anarchists have taken sides in armed conflicts between nations. Bakunin, for instance, championed the cause of France in the war of 1870–1 against Germany, and Kropotkin took a similar stand during the First World War, coming out in support of the Entente. *Kropotkin's action was prompted mainly by the fear that German militarism and authoritarianism might prove fatal to social progress in Europe. Moreover, as the bulwark of statism Germany blocked the path to the decentralized society of his dreams.*

In 1916 Kropotkin and other prominent anarchists – among them Jean Grave, Christian Cornelissen, Paul Reclus and Charles Malato – issued the Manifesto of the Sixteen in which they set forth their 'defencist' position. Despite the great prestige of their names, however, the majority of anarchists remained faithful to their anti-militarist heritage, rallying behind such 'internationalists' as Errico Malatesta, Alexander Berkman, Emma Goldman and Sébastien Faure. A group of Russian émigrés in Geneva, including Iuda Roshchin, Alexander Ge and Georgi Gogelia, branded Kropotkin and his associates as 'Anarcho-Patriots' and drafted the following reply which called for the conversion of the 'imperialist' war into a social revolution.

Reply *Geneva Group of Anarchist-Communists*

It will soon be two years since this terrible war began, a war such as humanity has never before experienced, yielding millions of nameless graves, millions of cripples, millions of widows and orphans. Billions of valuables, the products of long years of human toil, have been consigned to the flames, swallowed up by a bottomless abyss. Enormous sorrow, terrible suffering, the profound despair of humanity – all this is the result.

At this time, when cries of despair are audible everywhere – 'Enough bloodshed! Enough destruction!' – we look with deep sorrow upon our former comrades, P. Kropotkin, J. Grave, C. Cornelissen, P. Reclus, C. Malato and other anarchists and anti-militarists who declare in their recently published manifesto: 'No, there has been little bloodshed, little destruction. It is too early to talk of peace!'

In the name of what principles, for the sake of what ends have they found it possible to proclaim the necessity of fratricide? What has led such passionate adherents of peace to become the advocates of armed conflict? To us it is totally incomprehensible since, when reading their manifesto, one is struck by the wretchedness of that ideal in whose name they demand the continuation of the war to the end.

The authors of the manifesto declare that the guilty party in the war is Germany, which has set as its aim the annexation of Belgium and the

northern departments of France, has demanded of the latter heavy indemnities and intends in the future to seize its colonies. They reproach the German people for their obedience to their government and declare that so long as the population of Germany does not renounce the conquering schemes of its rulers there can be no talk of peace.

A clear partiality for the *Entente* pervades the whole manifesto. And this partiality, born of a gross overestimation of the dubious superiority of democratic regimes, has compelled the authors of the manifesto to remain silent about much that seriously compromises the Allied powers, to apply different criteria in evaluating identical actions of the belligerents, and finally to confuse the desires of the people with the desires of the governments that have enslaved them.

The signatories of the manifesto regard the German government as the guilty party in the war. But it is hardly a secret that all the great powers had long been preparing for a European war. And not merely for a defensive war, not merely to protect themselves against a German invasion. They were preparing, rather, for a war of conquest, for the conquest of new territory or for the economic domination of their neighbours. Has it not been a passionate dream of England to eliminate German rivalry on the seas? Isn't everyone well aware of Russia's desire to possess the shores of the Bosporus? Hasn't Russia turned a hungry eye towards Galicia? Has France ceased to dream of becoming a great colonial power?

All the states were preparing for war. And if war did not break out before 1914, it was only because the German Kiel Canal had not yet been widened, the construction of the English fleet had not yet been completed, the French army had not yet been perfected, nor new divisions yet created in Russia. And if, thanks to their organizational talents, the crowned pirates of Germany made preparations earlier than the others and decided before the others to set Europe in flames, this in no way diminishes the moral responsibility of the crowned pirates of England, Russia and the other states for the large number of victims who have been sacrificed on the altar of militarism.

The authors of the manifesto protest against the *possible* annexation by Germany of the territory it has occupied without the agreement of the people living there. But why have they not protested against the annexation of Egypt, an annexation *already carried out* by England during the course of the war and without the agreement of the Egyptian population? Why don't they issue a manifesto with a call for the workers to rise up against slave-holding England? Isn't it because such an act would pull the rug from under the feet of these anarcho-militarists? Would they not be obliged then to say clearly and distinctly that the present war is a war between two groups of predators equally inimical to freedom?

The authors of the manifesto are sure that to speak now of peace would be to encourage the designs of the German war party, which prepared the German invasion of its neighbouring states, an invasion that menaces all hopes of liberation and of human progress. We believe, however, that it is not the German invasion but the war as a whole, the responsibility for which falls equally on all states taking a direct or indirect part in it, that constitutes a threat to all hopes of liberation and to human progress. And we call upon the people to struggle not only against the German government but to rise against all their enslavers. We welcome the demonstrations at the Reichstag building by German women demanding peace and bread. All that is healthy and pure has manifested itself in these as yet feeble protests. We summon the toilers of all countries to stormy protests, to a popular uprising, because only by such means can we expect the regeneration of humanity, and not by the continuation of the war. The authors of the manifesto summon only the German people to revolt, while at the same time summoning the people of the Allied states to the trenches. Let them be consistent and reject both anti-militarism and revolution. For anti-militarism in France or revolutionary ferment in Russia or England will only benefit Germany. And any anti-militarism or revolution outside Germany will further the designs of the German war party. Yet this is precisely what Kropotkin has done. To our horror we have learned that even before the war he was opposed to the struggle against the law requiring three years of military service in France.

Do the authors of the manifesto really fail to understand that not only in the present war but in all wars one can find – in a purely formal sense – an allegedly greater or smaller degree of guilt, and that among the belligerents there will always be a greater or smaller degree of democracy? Thus they will always call on the less guilty to defend themselves; they will always remain slaves to the shameful slogan: 'Make the cannon and move them into position!'

Even now, as they shift from general phrases about progress and about the German menace to concrete declarations about the possible consequences of a German victory, they harbour only the fear that Germany might take France's colonies and reduce its neighbour to economic subjection in the guise of commercial agreements. And after all this Kropotkin and the other authors of the manifesto declare that they are anarchists and anti-militarists as before! Those who summon the people to war can be neither anarchists nor anti-militarists. They defend a cause which is alien to the toiling people. They would put the worker in the line of fire not in the name of his emancipation but for the glory of progressive national capitalism and of the state. They would tear up the spirit of anarchism and throw the pieces to the servants of militarism.

We, however, remain at our post. We appeal to the workers of the world to attack their immediate enemies, whoever their leaders may be – the German emperor or the Turkish sultan, the Russian tsar or the president of France. We know that, on the question of corrupting the will and conscience of labour, democracy and autocracy do not yield to each other. We make no distinction between acceptable or unacceptable wars. For us there exists only one war, the social war against capitalism and its defenders. And we repeat our old slogans which have been rejected by the authors of that shameful manifesto:

Down with the war!
Down with the rule of Authority and Capital!
Long live the brotherhood of free people!

Geneva Group of Anarchist-Communists

'Otvet', *Put' k Svobode* (Geneva), May 1917, pp. 10–11, first published in August 1916.

7 ANTI-INTELLECTUALISM

Anarchists have always set a high value on education (see Document 10), yet they have been deeply suspicious of elaborate philosophical systems and of the intellectuals who spin them. Ever since Bakunin they have rejected the notion that society is governed by rational laws, and have distrusted those who claim to possess superior wisdom or who preach so-called 'scientific' dogmas. In their eyes, the historical and sociological theories of Marx, Comte and others are nothing more than artificial contrivances which constrict the natural impulses of mankind. Some anarchists, indeed, have gone so far as to argue that intellectuals are a special breed who have nothing in common with manual labourers but try to lure them with high-flown formulas in order to catapult themselves into positions of privilege and authority.

The brothers A. L. and V. L. Gordin, the authors of Document 7b and probably of 7a as well, were leading proponents of this view. Passionate apostles of anti-intellectualism, they produced a steady stream of pamphlets and articles containing sweeping condemnations of European culture and its makers. In 1917 they founded a group called the Union of the Oppressed Five, with branches in Petrograd and Moscow, and worked out a philosophy of 'pan-anarchism' attacking the main institutions of social oppression. Anti-intellectualism lay at the root of the pan-anarchist creed. The Gordin brothers, decrying a priori *theories and scholastic abstractions, sought to liberate man's creative spirit from the shackles of dogma, whether of religion or science – for science, as they saw it, was merely a new religion used by the middle classes to dominate the unlettered masses.*

7a Proclamation

Homeless, shelterless son of the street, lured by the glow of the fireplace, the warmth and comforts of home, soft carpets underfoot, the lulling tones of a piano. All gates are closed to you. All doors are slammed shut. Your bare feet are cut by stones and ice, your ears pierced by the watchdog's howl and gatekeeper's shout. Bodies lounge on silken cushions – but   47 the wind cuts through your rags. Passions riot beneath warm blankets – but your lips are frozen, your heart is ashes, your hands are ice. You nestle yourself resignedly against a wall in some corner and doze fitfully. Nearby a prostitute walks back and forth. It's your daughter, selling her youthful flame to old hearts crusted with gold.

You stupid wretch! Right here is a home, here is warmth, here is comfort. Go in and settle down. Let the owners of the houses and palaces roam the streets and feel their own teeth chatter. Let their own daughters sell themselves if they refuse to build a new order on earth. Create Anarchy! Oppressed and smouldering people, ignite the flames of Anarchy. Let your life's blood, now grown cold, turn to the fire. Burn everything around you. Boldly ignite the flames of Anarchy. CREATE ANARCHY!

Rejected, fallen, despised ones, arise and destroy that society in which there is 'higher' and 'lower'. Arise and show that you are above us, that we are unworthy of your company, unworthy even of your contempt. Everything that was above you will be beneath you. Create Anarchy! Slaves, open your eyes and see that you are free! The deceivers are putting new chains on you. Fling them to the devil! Obey no one. Humble yourselves before no one. Create your own freedom, your own happiness. CREATE ANARCHY!

Uneducated ones, destroy that loathsome culture which divides men into 'ignorant' and 'learned'. They are keeping you in the dark. They have put out your eyes. And in this darkness, in the dark night of culture, they have robbed you.

People, the priests and scientists have robbed you, robbed you of your wholesome thoughts, your simplicity, your spontaneity, your feelings. Religion lies to you, people, and cunning science lies to you. The reign of heaven makes a fool of you; the priests deceive you; they trick you with a future order, a future socialism. The scientists and professors deceive you. Don't believe them. They hypnotize you and fleece you. They captivate you with the tawdry brilliance of their intellect.

People, your happiness is not in heaven but here on earth, not in the future but in the present. It lies in your own hands. Create Anarchy – completely, everywhere, and now. Destroy the churches, those nests of gentry lies; destroy the university, that nest of bourgeois lies. Drive away the priests, drive away the scientists! Destroy the false gentry and bourgeois heavens. Smash their Peruns,[1] gods and idols. There is only one god on earth: it is you, the people, you, Man.

People, you can be happy, you must be happy. CREATE ANARCHY!

From *Burevestnik* (Petrograd), 27 January 1918, p. 1.

[1] Perun: god of thunder and chief pagan deity of the eastern Slavs before the Christianization of Russia.

Pan-anarchism literally means all-embracing anarchism, 'pan' being 'all' in Greek. Pan-anarchism is a comprehensive and articulate anarchism. Aside from the ideal of no government, or anarchism proper, it entails four other ideals, namely: *communism*, with its 'everything belongs to everybody'; *pedism*, or the liberation of children and youth from the vice of servile education; *cosmism* (national-cosmopolitanism), the total emancipation of oppressed nationalities; and, finally, *gyneantropism*, that is, the emancipation and humanization of women. Taken together, these five ideals fall under the general heading of 'pan-anarchism'.

Pan-anarchism implies a synthesis (unification) of all the principal social ideals, actions and aspirations aiming towards a basic overthrow and reconstruction of *all* society – the economy, the family, the school, international relations and the institutions of government. In the economic sphere pan-anarchism entails the replacement of capitalism by communism, the abolition of private property in land, means of production and consumer goods. In the family it means the replacement of polygamy and the traffic in women by genuine love between individual man and woman, as well as the end of male domination of the family and of life as a whole, both in fact and in law, the free participation of women in all branches of labour and art and their equal enjoyment of all the benefits of society. In the school it means the replacement of present-day book learning, which indoctrinates our children and youth with religious and scientific prejudices, by a practical education in technical crafts which will be useful in everyday life and which will afford them freedom, self-reliance and the ability to create things by themselves with originality and independence of mind. It also means that the existing territorial system, with its fatherlands and state frontiers and national and private territorial ownership, will be replaced by a national-cosmopolitan order in which there are neither fatherlands nor frontiers but only free unions of free peoples to whom the whole earth belongs in common. 'The whole earth to all humanity' – such is the motto of pan-anarchism, as opposed to the territorialism and imperialism of predatory nations which declare that 'the whole earth is mine'.

In the realm of governmental organization and its relation to the individual, pan-anarchism stands for the elimination of authority, of the state, and of all forms of compulsion – courts, prisons, militias, etc. – and for the administration of society by means of voluntary agreements and consultation.

Pan-anarchism is the ideal of the Union of the Oppressed Five. It summons together all the oppressed to create a world-wide organization, an International of the Oppressed, a World Union of the Oppressed Five for the destruction of the existing order which is founded on five forms of oppression. Pan-anarchism takes the initiative in encouraging the unification of all five oppressed groups in contemporary society into a Worker-Vagabond International, a Youth International, an International of Oppressed Nationalities, a Women's International and an International of Individual Personalities, as well as the eventual formation of one joint International of the Oppressed founded on the principle of the *equality* of all the oppressed.

Pan-anarchism stands for pan-destruction, for the elimination of all five types of oppression in existing society. Thus the aim of pan-anarchism is not the liberation of one group of oppressed through the oppression of the rest, as for example in the inauguration of a dictatorship of the proletariat, but the liberation of all the oppressed, of all humanity, of all downtrodden elements. Pan-anarchism, moreover, is the liberation of humanity from the slavery of capitalism and the state, the slavery of formal education and of household drudgery, and the slavery of nationalism.

Pan-anarchism will destroy all five forms of oppression in contemporary society: (1) economic, (2) political, (3) national, (4) educational and (5) domestic. More simply, pan-anarchism insists that there be neither rich nor poor, neither rulers nor subjects, neither enslaving teachers nor enslaved pupils, neither male masters nor female slaves. For pan-anarchism each of these demands is of equal importance. Any superiority of one oppressed element over another, whether through leadership or domination, pan-anarchism brands as exploitation of human beings in favour of a particular class or group.

But pan-anarchism does not only mean emancipation from the five forms of oppression. It also means the emancipation of oppressed humanity from two deceptions: the deception of religion and the deception of science, which are in essence merely two varieties of the same deception, the deception of the oppressed by the oppressors. Pan-anarchism declares that religion and science were invented as a means of distracting attention from oppression and from the real tangible world, substituting for it an intangible world, either supernatural (religion) or abstract (science). Pan-anarchism views science as a reformed religion and nature as a reformed God. Science is the religion of the *bourgeoisie*, just as religion was the science of the nobility and slave-holders.

Pan-anarchism proclaims universal statelessness, cosmic anarchy, anarchy everywhere! All forms of religion and science are not only devices of bourgeois oppression, nets and snares, lures and bait for the oppressed. They are also fraudulent and barbarous, narrow and stupid, naïve and comical, muddled and contradictory. Science is one of the stupidities of the European savage, just as religion is a stupidity of the Asiatic savage. Both form a single tissue of confusions and contradictions: God and no God, cause and no cause; God the real builder and God building from 'nothing', meaning that he himself is the absolute 'nothing', a non-God; cause traced to the first cause, becoming self-cause or no cause.

God and Nature are made in man's image, anthropomorphic. The Eskimo envisages them from his hunting in the form of a white bear (the world originated from the white bear); the Hebrews from their trades (God the carpenter, the tailor). Newton, Kant and Laplace envisage Nature according to European mechanics, Darwin and Spencer according to English horse-breeding (natural selection followed the pattern of artificial selection in English horse-breeding). The rule of heaven and the rule of nature – angels, spirits, devils, molecules, atoms, ether, the laws of God/Heaven and the laws of Nature, forces, the influence of one body on another – all this is invented, formed, created by society (sociomorphic).

God is an image of the absolute Asian monarch. The laws of heaven, the laws of the stars, the astrology of Assyria and Babylonia – these are the laws of emperors. The laws of Nature are the laws of the state; natural force is coercion. The forces of Nature resemble the European constitutional monarchs and constitutional bureaucracy, and sometimes Nature even resembles the president of a democratic republic!

Pan-anarchism teaches that the universe is neither man nor society. It has neither beginning nor end, neither origin (cosmogony) nor cause, neither laws nor knout-like forces. The universe and every natural phenomenon is always 'itself', anarchist-individualist or anarchist-communist, so to speak. The universe and all its phenomena are spontaneous. In the universe and in every phenomenon there is nothing external, no coercive order, but rather *anarchy*, i.e. internal (immanent) order, independent and spontaneous. There is no natural force but only actions and affinities; and things, actions and affinities are identical.

For pan-anarchism the basic error of religion and science is that the first is the fruit of fantasy and the second the fruit of the intellect (mental configurations or abstractions). Thus pan-anarchism holds only feelings, or rather muscles and technics, to be genuine. Pan-anarchism regards only technics as the culture of the people, the toilers, the oppressed, technics in the broad meaning of the term, embracing all crafts, all practical arts, and so on, which it calls pan-technics.

With regard to the study of society, pan-anarchism rejects all sociological laws or social evolution and development, replacing these with *socio-technics*, the building of society with the explicit right of social experimentation, improvisation and invention. Pan-anarchism, clothed in technicalism, means not only total and universal anarchy but also anarchy now. Instead of Social-Democratic evolution and reform, it advances the slogan of Social Revolution, upholding the golden anarchist rule: Straight on towards our goal!

And so –

Long live Pan-anarchy!

A. L. and V. L. Gordin, *Manifest pananarkhistov* (Moscow, 1918), 3–6.

The violent rejection of the past which characterizes the theory of pan-anarchism is even more pronounced in the manifesto of the Anarcho-Futurists, a group based in the southern city of Kharkov, a major anarchist centre during the Civil War period. Like the Gordin brothers, the Anarcho-Futurists invented a new vocabulary to suit the post-bourgeois era in the making. With Bakunin they were apostles of universal destruction, sharing his belief that 'the passion to destroy is a creative passion', and that a new world would emerge from the ruins of the old. In their contempt for the old and exaltation of the new, their deliberate effort to shock and outrage, and their call for the wholesale destruction of art and culture, they echoed the celebrated Futurist Manifesto *published in 1909 by Filippo Marinetti. At times, indeed, their language is nearly identical with that of Marinetti, with its unrestrained imagery and cascading metaphors: 'Italy has been the great second-hand market for too long. We want to get rid of the innumerable museums which cover it with innumerable cemeteries. . . . Let the good incendiaries with charred fingers come! Here they are! Heap up the fire to the shelves of the libraries! Direct the canals to flood the cellars of the museums! Let the glorious canvases swim ashore! Take the picks and hammers! Undermine the foundation of venerable towns!'* [1]

7c Anarcho-Futurist Manifesto

Ah-ah-ah, ha-ha, ho-ho!

Fly into the streets! All who are still fresh and young and not dehumanized – to the streets! The pot-bellied mortar of laughter stands in a square drunk with joy. Laughter and Love, copulating with Melancholy and Hate, pressed together in the mighty, convulsive passion of bestial lust. Long live the psychology of contrasts! Intoxicated, burning spirits have raised the flaming banner of intellectual revolution. Death to the creatures of routine, the philistines, the sufferers from gout! Smash with a deafening noise the cup of vengeful storms! Tear down the churches and their allies the museums! Blast to smithereens the fragile idols of Civilization! Hey, you decadent architects of the sarcophagi of thought, you watchmen of the universal cemetery of books – stand aside! We have come to remove you! The old must be buried, the dusty archives burned by the Vulcan's torch of creative genius. Past the flaky ashes of world-wide devastation, past the charred canvases of bulky paintings, past the burned, fat, pot-bellied volumes of classics we march, we Anarcho-Futurists! Above the vast

[1] James Joll, *Three Intellectuals in Politics* (New York, 1960), pp. 179–84.

expanse of devastation covering our land the banner of anarchy will be proudly unfurled. Writing has no value! There is no market for literature! There are no prisons, no limits for subjective creativity! Everything is permitted! Everything is unrestricted!

The Children of Nature receive in joyous ecstasy the chivalrous golden kiss of the Sun and the lascivious, naked, fat belly of the Earth. The Children of Nature springing from the black soil kindle the passions of naked, lustful bodies. They press them all in one spawning, pregnant cup! Thousands of arms and legs are welded into a single suffocating exhausted heap! The skin is inflamed by hot, insatiable, gnawing caresses. Teeth sink with hatred into warm succulent lovers' flesh! Wide, staring eyes follow the pregnant, burning dance of lust! Everything is strange, uninhibited, elemental. Convulsions – flesh – life – death – everything! Everything!

Such is the poetry of our love! Powerful, immortal, and terrible are we in our love! The north wind rages in the heads of the Children of Nature. Something frightful has appeared – some vampire of melancholy! Perdition – the world is dying! Catch it! Kill it! No, wait! Frenzied, penetrating cries

Delegates to the First All-Russian Congress of Soviets, June 1917. This new authority was nearly as antipathetic to the more extreme anarchists as the tsarist regime had been.

pierce the air. Wait! Melancholy! Black yawning ulcers of agony cover the pale, terror-stricken face of heaven. The earth trembles with fear beneath the mighty wrathful blows of its Children! Oh, you cursed, loathsome things! They tear at its fat, tender flesh and bury their withered, starving melancholy in the flowing blood and fresh wounds of its body. The world is dying! Ah! Ah! Ah! cry millions of tocsins. Ah! Ah! Ah! roar the giant cannon of alarm. Destruction! Chaos! Melancholy! The world is dying!

Such is the poetry of our melancholy! We are uninhibited! Not for us the wailing sentimentality of the humanists. Rather, we shall create the triumphant intellectual brotherhood of peoples, forged with the iron logic of contradictions, of Hate and Love. With bared teeth we shall protect our free union, from Africa to the two poles, against any sentimental level of friendship. Everything is ours! Outside us is only death! Raising the black flag of rebellion, we summon all living men who have not been dehumanized, who have not been benumbed by the poisonous breath of Civilization! All to the streets! Forward! Destroy! Kill! Only death admits no return! Extinguish the old! Thunder, lightning, the elements – all are ours! Forward!

Long live the international intellectual revolution!

An open road for the Anarcho-Futurists, Anarcho-Hyperboreans, and Neo-Nihilists!

Death to world Civilization!

Group of Anarcho-Futurists

'Shturmovoi, opustoshaiushchii manifest anarkho-
futuristov', *K Svetu* (Kharkov), 14 March 1919, p. 1.

8 INDIVIDUALISM

The Individualist Anarchists were opposed to every form of authority which might limit their personal freedom. For them society was nothing more than a collection of autonomous individuals, and they were deeply suspicious of all types of organization, even those put forward by their fellow anarchists. Strongly influenced by Max Stirner and Benjamin Tucker, the German and American theorists of Individualist anarchism, they demanded the total liberation of the human personality from the fetters of organized society. In their view, even the voluntary communities of Bakunin and Kropotkin might restrict the freedom of the individual. From Nietzsche, moreover, the Individualists inherited a desire for a complete overthrow of all middle-class values, political, moral and cultural. Some Individualists found the ultimate expression of their social alienation in terrorism or crime, others attached themselves to avant-garde literary and artistic circles, but the majority remained 'philosophical' anarchists who conducted animated parlour discussions and elaborated their theories in ponderous journals and books.

Document 8a, by the prolific Gordin brothers, is a brief statement of the

Individualist position which concludes with a famous dictum of Stirner, the fore-most prophet of the Individualist creed: 'There is no authority higher than myself' (Mir geht nichts über mich). *The next selection is by A. A. Borovoi, a scholarly anarchist who sought to reconcile his Individualism with other streams of anarchist thought and who, in contrast to the Gordins, held Western culture in high esteem.*

8a Nothing Forgotten and Nothing Learned

A. L. and V. L. GORDIN

The unwillingness of the common people to rule over others and their desire, on the contrary, to abolish authority; their refusal to obey or to grovel; their instinctive tendency towards anarchy, to secure a true dictator-ship of the proletariat rather than a fictitious one in the form of Executive Committees or Soviets, a dictatorship, that is, of the people themselves, the power of each person over himself – this is the true dictatorship of the Individual. I am my own minister, my own lawmaker, my own dictator, my own authority. This is a real popular dictatorship, a natural, normal, physiological dictatorship. It is the most natural thing for an individual to possess physiological power, to exercise a physiological dictatorship over the parts of his body, over his arms and legs, to dictate his own behaviour through the power of free action, the power to do what he feels is neces-sary. This is the physiological, the only proper, natural and just dictatorship of free activity. This is the ideal of Anarchy.

I am a person – and there is no authority higher than my 'I'!

Br. Gordiny, 'Nichego ne zabyli i nichemu ne nauchilis'',
Anarkhist (Rostov-on-Don), 22 October 1917, pp. 1–2,
abridged.

8b Anarchist Manifesto   A. A. BOROVOI

Revolution and freedom have always been born in blood and suffering. They have claimed many victims, both the heroic fighters for the new and the desperate defenders of the old. But these victims shall not have fallen in vain. Before us lies a gigantic labour such as humanity has never yet known. It is necessary to rebuild the whole country, which has been shattered by the corruption of the old regime, by the war, and by the experiments 'from above' of various political parties. This reconstruction must inaugurate not the old routine, not the musty dogmatism of the professional conjurers of human happiness, but something new and creative, taken directly from life and answering the desires and interests of those by and for whom the revolution was made.

It is time to make an end to every guardianship, however well-intentioned. It is time to make an end to representation, no matter who the representatives may be. Each individual must take his own cause in his own hands. It is this to which anarchism summons us!

Anarchism is the doctrine of life! Anarchism is born and lives in each person, but is crushed by poverty, timidity and servility before men and theories tending towards a violent and corrupt life. What is needed is courage, enlightenment and a thirst for action, so that in everyone, great and small alike, the spirit of anarchism will awaken.

Anarchism is the doctrine of freedom! Not abstract, illusory freedom, but alive and real. At the root of all anarchist creativity lies the free personality, free from the yoke of institutions and from the authority of laws invented by others. The anarchist's freedom is the freedom of all. If there is but a single slave, the anarchist is not free. The anarchist must struggle until all men are free. For anarchism there are no idols, no absolutes except man himself, his freedom and his right to unrestricted development. No matter what the social order may be, the anarchist will continue to strive towards a new, more perfect, fuller and purer one dictated by his libertarian conscience.

Anarchism is the doctrine of equality! All are equal in freedom. Each is the maker of his own destiny. And the sphere of his personal freedom is inviolable.

Anarchism is the doctrine of culture! For it teaches not merely love for oneself or one's personal freedom but love for all and freedom for all. It is a call to action, to the great task of making its fruits available not only to our contemporaries but to our brothers of the still distant future. It is a call to fight for the destruction of the coercive system, but not a call to vengeance or to mob law against certain specific individuals.

Anarchism is the doctrine of happiness! For it believes in man and his boundless possibilities. It believes that by acting for all he will link together all ages and all men. Thus is born the joy of creation – the greatest of all joys for man!

A. A. Borovoi, 'Anarkhistskii manifest', in his *Anarkhizm* (Moscow, 1918), 168–9.

9 ANARCHIST YOUTH

A striking feature of the anarchist movement was the youthfulness of its adherents. Many anarchists were drawn from the high schools and universities, so that nineteen or twenty was a fairly typical age and some of the most active militants were only sixteen or seventeen. Their objectives are summarized in the following proclamation issued in 1919 by the Young Anarchists of the Nabat *(Alarm)* Confederation, *the largest anarchist organization in the Ukraine.*

Group of young anarchists in Moscow during the Russian Civil War.

Comrades!

Wednesday, 16 April 1919

COMRADES!

The revolutionary horizons are broadening. The oppressed are growing more and more powerful on their road to liberation. Their chains are falling off, their fetters are breaking, and all that is decrepit and unfit for the new life is being swept out of the way.

On the banner of liberation is written:

A struggle against all oppressors.

A struggle against all who have made learning a privilege of the few and steeped it in lies to benefit the mighty.

A struggle against all institutions that cripple us in childhood and youth, that turn us into anaemic, pale and stunted creatures cowed in body and spirit.

A struggle against that society which has imprisoned us in factories and schools.

A struggle against the existing family, which has turned us into deceitful hypocrites nourished on the poison of corruption.

57

A struggle against state authority, which fosters oppression and inequality.

This is what we young anarchists put forward as the basis of our appeal. A large part of youth, having been nourished on the poison of bourgeois philistinism, regard the situation in which they find themselves as normal. Our duty is to rouse them from their hibernation so that they can join our ranks for creative work. So hasten to productive work. Hasten to apply to life those ideals which life itself has put forward!

We, the youth of the Ukraine, having organized ourselves in circles, must be united for the sake of efficient and productive work. In the name of mutual aid and solidarity – those powerful engines of human progress – such unity is essential. And to achieve it we must summon a congress of all groups of anarchist youth of the Ukraine. The congress must examine many vital questions whose urgency will admit no delay.

Let the black flag, beneath which we stand, come to signify the destruction and death of all the old and rotten institutions which have enslaved us! Let the strength of our words and our common aspirations unite all youth now scattered and isolated from revolutionary creativity.

Let our road be the road of cultural and social creativity. And our call shall be the slogan: Youth of the world unite for revolutionary and cultural work!

STEP LIVELY TO ACTION!

Organizational Group for Summoning an All-Ukrainian Congress of Anarchist Youth

'Tovarishchi!' *Biulleten' Initsiativnoi gruppy anarkhistov molodezhi Ukrainy 'Nabat'* (Kharkov), April 1919, p. 1.

10 EDUCATION

To prepare men for the libertarian society of the future, the anarchists pinned their greatest hopes on education. Inspired by the teachings of Kropotkin, Tolstoy and Francisco Ferrer, they called for an 'integrated education' that would cultivate both mental and manual skills in a libertarian atmosphere, free from the domination of church or state. Due emphasis was to be placed on the humanities and on the basic principles of mathematics and science, but instead of being taught from books alone the students were to receive an active outdoor education and learn by doing and observing at first hand, a programme that has been endorsed by many 'progressive' educational theorists. The following resolution, which embodies some of these principles, was adopted by the Second All-Russian Conference of Anarcho-Syndicalists, which met in Moscow in November and December 1918.

Theses on the Cultural Organization of Russia

In the area of culture and education the Second All-Russian Conference of Anarcho-Syndicalists sets as its goals:

A To awaken interest among the proletarian masses in art, learning and cultural pursuits.

B To seek ways and means of developing the initiative and creativity of the masses. This will help improve conditions within the framework of the present bourgeois state socialist order. It will also make it possible for the proletariat to create its own socialist – as opposed to bourgeois – culture and its own art, which will reflect the shining beauty and magnificence of stateless socialism and open to the human mind the widest prospects and possibilities.

C To encourage in every way possible the development of the individual personality, with all its disparate features, eliminating prejudices and pre-conceived ideas while seeking to present facts which will help the individual formulate his own opinions about things.

D To impress upon the proletarian masses the idea that they must rely only on their own forces in all their activities, holding fast to the golden words enshrined in the memory of the First International: 'The liberation of the workers is the task of the workers themselves.'

E To apply every means to inculcate in the proletarian masses the habit of thinking independently, since the strongest convictions are those which we arrive at ourselves.

F To help the workers teach themselves self-respect and to know how to make others respect them, not only without laws but in spite of them and in spite of 'the world of power' around us.

G To nurture within the proletarian army a strong will and a firm mind; to nurture among the workers the spirit of revolt and to make of them conscious, loyal, tireless and fearless fighters in the true spirit of relentless class struggle for a shining future, for anarchism.

H To unite all proletarian organizations and to stimulate their development in every way.

I To satisfy all inquiries in the fields of learning and art by organizing truly proletarian institutions – universities, theatres, libraries, reading rooms, schools of different types, proletarian palaces, museums, conservatories, etc.

J The activities of Anarcho-Syndicalism must therefore aim for the elimination of power, compulsion, and authority.

K To encourage the development of the above-mentioned institutions, by means of which the proletariat must wrest from the arms of the state and church the entire function of education and learning and take it in its own hands.

As a result, all cultural and educational activities of Anarcho-Syndicalism will rest:

A On the self-discipline of the proletariat, and not on discipline taught by lies and dissimulation.

B On the removal of all compulsory programmes which level all individual characteristics and personal traits and kill the spirit of initiative, self-reliance and responsibility.

Education will thus become:

1 Many-sided but integrated, offering the chance to achieve the harmonious development of the whole personality by giving it something whole, complete, and related to every area of art and science.

2 Rational, founded on reason and corresponding to the latest discoveries of science rather than on blind faith; on the development of personal dignity and independence rather than on a feeling of submission or obedience; on the elimination of stories about God, which are false and harmful to the cause of the peasants' and workers' liberation.

3 Co-educational, the joint teaching of both sexes so as to remove coarse ideas and to ensure a higher morality that will advance the cause of women far more than all the laws put together, laws which have been directed towards their total enslavement.

4 Libertarian, abandoning the idea of power for the principle of freedom, because the aim of cultural and educational activity is the development of free men who cherish not only their own freedom but also the freedom of others.

For the success of this great task of instruction and education, if it is to be truly revolutionary rather than mere cultural dilettantism, it is necessary to give all cultural and educational organizations of peasants and workers full freedom and autonomy in their own immediate bailiwick. But they must in turn advance towards a free federation of city, township, district and provincial centres concerned with technical, cultural and educational questions which, owing to their importance, reach beyond the narrow circle of local organizations and affect the interests of peasant and worker educational organizations at all levels: city, township, district, province, region, and the whole country.

These organizations and centres must replace the existing state apparatus which monopolizes all cultural and educational work.

Vmesto programmy: rezoliutsii I i II Vserossiiskikh
konferentsii anarkho-sindikalistov (Berlin, 1922), 23–5.

11 THE FUTURE SOCIETY

Anarchists have generally been reluctant to provide a detailed blueprint of the future Utopia. Yet, as the following selections show, they did attempt to sketch at least its general outlines. Nearly all anarchists envisioned a decentralized society based on the voluntary cooperation of free individuals, a society without government or property, without hunger or want, in which men would direct their own affairs unimpeded by any authority. For most anarchists the natural framework for such a society was a loose federation of self-governing communes, both urban and rural, the nature of which is analysed in Document 11a by Nikolai Pavlov, a leader of the Moscow Union of Bakers.

Beyond this, however, there was little agreement. For some anarchists the golden age meant a return to a simpler past, before large-scale industry began to transform human beings into an army of faceless robots. They longed to recapture the direct human relationships of the medieval commune and the handicrafts cooperative and to restore a primitive bliss in which there was neither tsar nor state but only land and liberty. A majority, however, welcomed technical progress, convinced that up-to-date machinery would relieve men of drudgery and fatigue, allow time for leisure and cultural pursuits, and remove the stigma traditionally attached to manual labour. Such is the position of A. Grachev, the author of selection 11b. A Petrograd Syndicalist, he scorned the romantic visionaries who pined for pastoral Utopias, oblivious of the complex forces at work in the modern world. To spurn mechanized industry merely because it was born of the capitalist system was in his view the greatest folly. In the future society, rather, millions of workers would live happily in large cities and work in modern factories which they themselves would administer. In this way the labourer would regain the dignity of being his own master, without sacrificing the gains of modern science and technology.

11a The Free Commune and the Free City N. I. PAVLOV

Each day we see new evidence that the number of peasant communes is growing. This is entirely understandable. For the social life of the people has till now been artificially and forcibly broken up by the government and capitalism, and this fact, compounded by the destruction caused by the world-wide slaughter of peoples, has compelled the poorest peasants to take refuge in the communal working of the land. Turning our attention to the peasant communes, which have been created in local districts owing to the demands of life itself, we would like to explain to the toilers our conception of the free anarchist commune of the future society.

The free commune is a union of producers, consumers and distributors united according to trade and sometimes also to mutual sympathies. In addition, this union for the purpose of independent activity and organized creativity is called into being by other mutual needs of all sorts. The anarchist commune, as a self-governing and autonomous unit of labour, a unit of social production, enters into close ties with other free labour communes. Together they form, from the bottom up, a federation of communes. All communes united in such a federation arrange for an exchange of products, by which each commune, in return for its available surpluses, receives those products which it lacks. All this is done by free accord and mutual agreement. There can be no talk of a law-making body for the communes or their federation, for that would lead to the decline and fall of the communes.

We are not state socialists, not communist Bolsheviks who seize power in their hands and, proceeding from the top, artificially and forcibly introduce communism by laws and decrees, enforcing all their decisions (whether good or bad) by every available means, including the use of armed force. The state communists retort: 'Yes, that's all very well. But we are not much interested in what will happen in the future. That's the business of future generations. Show us concretely how at this time we can organize an anarchist commune, even in a limited way.' To which we reply that the anarchist commune, in the full meaning of the term, is not now conceivable. What *is* possible, however, is for workers' organizations to struggle towards anarchist communism by demolishing all state barriers standing in the way of its realization.

Having begun the struggle, we can now start to organize the free commune, at least in a rudimentary way. We say that state communism has nothing in common with anarchist communism, and we thus assert categorically that to arrive at freedom through state socialism (as the socialists claim) is unthinkable. For state communism is authoritarian, and the way to state communism lies in nationalization, whereby all the means of production and exchange belong not to autonomous workers' unions but to the state. The state takes everything in its own hands, not only the enterprises but even the workers' organizations. It completely monopolizes everything, including even art and literature, and seeks to establish not socialism but state communism, replacing the capitalist exploiters with one giant, one all-smashing fist, the state. State communism does not intend to abolish the state system of force and compulsion but only to reshape it by replacing the old bourgeois state forms with new ones, with a state communist order.

We Anarcho-Syndicalists oppose collectivism (state communism) with free anarchist communism, which recognizes the right of man to his own life and to the full satisfaction of all his needs. This right is seen not as vulgar huckstering, not as an exchange for a specific quantity of labour, but as the participation of each individual, according to his strength, in productive life. This demand is expressed in the formula which anarchist communism puts at the root of free organization: 'From each according to his ability, to each according to his needs.' Stateless communism envisions that all products and tools of production and exchange will pass directly to the common ownership of the workers' and peasants' producers' unions and communes.

Anarchist communism abolishes all centralized authority and seeks to achieve decentralization by smashing the state into a multitude of autonomous and independent labouring groups and communes, which hitherto have been artificially tied together by state compulsion. For the solution of problems affecting several communes, the free commune will choose delegations of specialists on practical questions who will receive instructions from the whole commune. The commune itself will make all decisions on the basis of a report of the results of a meeting of these specialists.

As for the free city, we believe that for the purpose of production and distribution this organization must take the form of a union-communal organization. In the free city a mass of communes will be formed and joined together into unions of producers' groups organized according to trade. These groups will hold in their hands all the expropriated tools of production and exchange and will work in close harmony with one another. At the moment of the fundamental break, and with the transition from capitalist society to free communism, factory and peasant committees aided by craft unions will play a key role in the organization of production and distribution on new lines.

As Syndicalists, we see the nucleus of the first producers' groups in the revolutionary syndicates. At the moment of social upheaval (Syndicalist revolution) and of the proclamation of the city as free, its life and activity will be greatly eased by the reorganization of production. The function of food distribution will be assumed by cooperatives and house committees, which will be united in street, block, district, and finally city committees. These will handle the distribution of basic necessities and decide all questions concerning food, clothing and shelter.

In the free commune or group, discipline will not be imposed by anyone but will be conscious self-discipline. The communes must be living entities. All their members must be dedicated practical workers, applying their maximum effort and influencing others by their example. The main goal of each commune must be the full and free development of the human personality. Within the commune mutual aid will be practised in all areas of life: production, distribution, defence from external attack, and so on.

The anarchist commune is completely free and chooses, without outside interference, its administration or council, which will act as the executive commission of the commune but nothing more. Each commune organizes itself naturally, in accordance with local conditions, and will if necessary dissolve itself by its own decision.

N. I. Pavlov, 'Svobodnaia kommuna i vol'nyi gorod',
Vol'nyi Golos Truda (Moscow), 16 September 1918, pp. 2–3.

Their opponents reproach the anarchists with Utopianism, with abstractness. The anarchist ideal is depicted by its enemies as a Utopia based on the return to handicrafts production and a natural economy. One must admit that the occasion for such attacks is often provided by the anarchists themselves, anarchists who have not clearly mastered the social and economic principles on which a libertarian society is to be built. Of the winged words of the rebel Bakunin – that the urge to destroy is also a creative urge – many present-day anarchists have only a superficial or two-dimensional understanding. In the opinion of such anarchists, contemporary production with its giant industry and millions of workers – servants of the machine – must be destroyed and refashioned anew. However, they provide no precise idea of the extent to which mechanized production, concentrated in the cities, must be eliminated and what will replace it in the future. We shall try to shed some light on these questions.

In the realm of political ideals anarchism means simply anarchy, that is, the absence of authority. In the social and economic realm this stateless ideal rests in communism. The basic social and economic cell of the anarchist society is the free, independent commune. But what is meant by the commune as the basic cell of the future society? The first and most important misconception one encounters when raising this question, even among the anarchists themselves, is the linking of the notion of a 'commune' with the idea of a social unit tied to a definite territory and strictly defined territorially. Here the commune coincides with the rural village, with a specific agricultural or other economic unit run by a group of people on communist lines.

The second misconception, closely related to the first, is that such a territorially distinct commune is viewed as an independent and self-sufficient economic organism, satisfying by itself (so far as possible) all the needs of its members.

The result of these two misconceptions is an image of the anarchist society as one in which humanity is divided – depending on the individual peculiarities of separate peoples – into greater or smaller communities, entirely independent of one another and, so far as possible, serving their own particular needs. Such a conception of the anarchist ideal, however, implies the negation of existing forms of production and exchange, the revival of a natural economy and scattered handicrafts production, and the cessation of the distribution of manufactured goods throughout the whole society.

It is hardly necessary to say that such a conception of the anarchist society is completely erroneous. Indeed, it is precisely this conception of anarchism that its opponents have in mind when they reproach anarchists with Utopian and even petty bourgeois beliefs. Yet it cannot be denied that the above interpretation of anarchist society is partly the fault of the theorists of anarchism themselves, who have insufficiently worked out the position of anarchists on the legacy which survives from capitalism. A particularly inaccurate appraisal of the significance of the capitalist legacy for the future society has been fostered by the works of Kropotkin, in which he strongly emphasizes the tendency towards decentralization in contemporary production. What one merely desires has been accepted as fact. A tendency towards decentralization in industry has been prematurely discerned and exaggerated, creating the impression that in the future society everything that is needed by members of a commune will be produced on the spot by the efforts of the commune itself.

The first misconception – tying the commune to a given area – has been widely disseminated in anarchist theoretical works. Yet the commune, which forms the basis of the future society, is not necessarily tied to a particular territory. The commune is simply a union of people for joint work to attain common goals. Any such union, for whatever purpose it may be founded and however great or insignificant it may be, however broad or limited its activities, constitutes a commune. Such a commune not tied to a given territorial framework is called an extraterritorial commune. And it is this extraterritorial commune which forms the social and economic base of the anarchist society. The relations of such communes with one another for the purpose of satisfying mutual needs are complex and closely intertwined, so that the communes are interrelated in all spheres, thereby constituting a single, indivisible social fabric.

The second misconception which has given ammunition to the superficial critics of anarchism – the link between the anarchist social ideal and the handicrafts mode of production – is closely tied to the first, but for a full clarification it must be explored from a slightly different angle. To elucidate this question we must discuss openly and distinctly the question of our attitude towards authority after the passing of contemporary capitalism. Is it true that by destroying the bourgeois system the anarchists will also tamper with the industrial system of contemporary society? On the day after their victory will the anarchists preserve the legacy of capitalism, or will they turn their backs on it and begin to create new and different economic forms? Will the anarchists leave untouched those human anthills, the giant factories and plants? Will there possibly be, in the anarchist society, enterprises in which tens of thousands of men will work together under the same roof? Will these urban giants retain their powers of attraction and draw the populace into their magnetic tentacles? Will we preserve in the anarchist society the division of labour and large-scale mechanized production?

Here are the questions whose answers will provide an accurate conception of the future society. Let us say in advance that to reject out of hand everything that capitalism has created in the realm of production and distribution would be a harmful Utopia, fatal for anarchism. In the realm of production and exchange we must be the perpetuators of capitalism. We must not reject the capitalist heritage but clasp it whole to ourselves. In the system of production created by capitalism there are many positive features, progressive from the standpoint of human development. We shall not use our victory to return mankind to a primitive condition. Taking production in our hands, we shall destroy not a single machine nor damage a single lever. We shall not abandon our factories and plants nor replace them with an idyllic life in huts in fields and forests under the open sky.

On the contrary, we shall bring our liberated energy to the factory. We shall imbue our machines with new power. We shall build as yet unheard-of giants from concrete, glass and steel. We shall raise industry to new and untouched heights. Our cities shall not be broken up and dispersed. Rather they will blossom with gardens, and additional millions of people will joyously fill their sunlit streets.

The anarchist society will not disperse production but consolidate it even further. With steel rails and steamship lines we shall link together the remotest corners of the earth and vastly expand and revitalize trade. We shall build new workshops, but such as can be filled by many thousands of workmen together.

It is thus that the future society must be envisaged by those who have correctly grasped the trends of the present and who have escaped the clutches of obsolescence. But what place will the commune occupy in this future society? What will it become? What sort of organizations will assume the task of fulfilling the needs of such a society? Is it not obvious that a decisive role in the life of such a society, marching forward and not backward from the present, will belong to the unions which handle production? The whole society will rest on powerful producers' unions linked together by economic ties dictated by production itself.

The vague conception of the commune as the social and economic basis of society thus acquires a well-defined content. The commune of the future society is the workers' union of production or distribution. Thus Anarchist-Communists, in their work, must not lose sight of the fact that the workers' unions in the realm of production are in essence those very communes on which the future edifice of anarchist communism will be built.

A. Grachev, 'Anarkhicheskii kommunizm', *Golos Truda*
(Petrograd), 15 September 1917, pp. 3–4.

'The Bourgeois Order', a cartoon by Robert Minor from the organ of the
Petrograd Federation of Anarchist-Communists, Kommuna, September 1917.
It originally appeared in The Blast (15 January 1916), published by
Alexander Berkman in San Francisco.

Part Three
Workers' Control

The Russian Revolution, like the Spanish Civil War, was one of the few instances in modern history when workers' control was put into practice on a wide scale. For the most part, however, 'control' did not entail the actual seizure and management of the factories by the workers themselves. What it meant, rather, was that local factory committees took part in fixing wages, hours and working conditions, supervised the hiring and firing of labour, and in general kept watch over the activities of the factory administration. In some cases the workers ejected unpopular directors, engineers and foremen and took upon themselves the tasks of management, but this was the exception rather than the rule.

Although workers' control was endorsed by the Bolsheviks in the spring of 1917, its most vigorous and consistent champions were the Anarcho-Syndicalists, who pinned their hopes on the factory committees both to overthrow the capitalist system and to become the nuclei of the future libertarian society. The principal Syndicalist journal in Russia was Golos Truda *(The Voice of Labour), edited by Volin and with G.P. Maksimov, a member of the Central Council of Factory Committees, as one of its leading contributors.* Golos Truda *served as the organ of the Petrograd Union of Anarcho-Syndicalist Propaganda, which spread the Syndicalist gospel among the workers of the capital, and whose founding declaration of 4 June 1917 appears as Document 12.*

The Anarcho-Syndicalists exercised a significant influence among the bakers, river transport, dock and shipyard workers, Donets miners (who adopted the preamble to the IWW constitution as their programme), food industry workers, postal and telegraph workers, and, to a lesser extent, metal and textile workers, printers and railwaymen. But, as Maksimov's article shows (Document 13), they were critical of the traditional trade unions, which were mostly dominated by the Social Democrats and which, to the Syndicalists, represented vestiges of a moribund capitalist order. Rather it was the 'bold' and 'truly revolutionary' factory committees, insisted Maksimov and his colleagues, which would sweep away the Provisional Government and usher in a shining new era of direct proletarian democracy.

12 Declaration of the Petrograd Union of Anarcho-Syndicalist Propaganda

The present moment represents a turning point in the history of mankind. The world war, which has already been raging for three years, has revealed

Above, *poster explaining the establishment of workers' control in the factories and the formation of guard patrols to protect workers' interests from the grasping hands of the church, thieves and the capitalist class. Another poster, 'The Red Ploughman' (below), glamorizes the Russian peasant, who is shown majestically ploughing into the land the symbols of authority and capitalism.*

with striking clarity the total collapse of the foundations on which contemporary society rests. The clearest testimony to the downfall of the capitalist order is the popular revolution which has erupted throughout Russia and which continues to develop in the direction of a fundamental social overturn. In addition, there is the ferment among the proletariat of other capitalist countries, which must sooner or later assume the proportions of a mass revolutionary upheaval. These historical events are of the first importance. They show that the advance guard of the international proletariat, which has been seeking a way out of the intolerable situation arising from the three-year war launched by the imperialist *bourgeoisie* of the great powers, is suddenly faced with the prospect of a full-scale social revolution, which hitherto seemed a matter for the distant future.

The need for a basic social and economic reconstruction is at present felt particularly keenly by the proletariat of Russia. The great disorganization of the economic life of the country, the complete bankruptcy towards which Russia is rapidly moving and which is unavoidable if the inviolability of capitalist forms is to be allowed to persist, requires the immediate organization by the working masses themselves of new forms of economic relations. No social reforms carried out from above by a bourgeois, semi-socialist or even completely socialist Provisional Government or Constituent Assembly can alleviate the economic plight which is growing worse each day. Popular organizations – organizations of the workers and peasants – must not rely on reforms from above but must undertake a direct and fundamental reorganization of contemporary social and economic relationships.

Such an organization is already present to a significant extent. On the very morrow of the overthrow of the house of Romanovs there began a feverish organization of labour at the grass-roots level. The Anarcho-Syndicalists, having always set great hopes on the creative spirit of the masses and on their capacity for self-organization during a revolutionary situation, were not disappointed in their expectations. The whole expanse of Russia is now covered by an intricate network of popular organizations: soviets of peasants', workers' and soldiers' deputies, industrial unions, factory committees, unions of landless peasants, etc., etc. And with each day the conviction is growing among the toiling masses that only the people themselves, through their own non-party organizations, can accomplish the task of a fundamental social and economic reconstruction.

The state has already been dealt the first crushing blow. It must now be replaced by an all-Russian federation of free cities and free communes, by urban and rural communes united from the bottom up in local, district, and regional federations. Such a political reconstruction will provide a radical solution to the question of full autonomy for small territorial units. It will also point the way to the solution of complex national questions, which could not be solved so long as the state – even if 'democratic' in allowing a measure of autonomy to the nationalities – was preserved. The soviets of workers', peasants' and soldiers' deputies, expressing the political will of the masses, must take upon themselves the execution of this political reconstruction of the country on the basis of the widest introduction of federalism.

But the execution of a second and even more important task, that of *a total economic reconstruction*, must be left to other popular organizations better fitted for the purpose: industrial unions and other economic organizations of workers and peasants. The confiscation of the land, workers' control over production and further steps towards the complete socialization of the land and the factories can be undertaken only by federations of unions of labouring peasants, industrial unions, factory committees, control commissions and the like in local districts throughout the country. Only an all-Russian union of these organizations of producers, around which will also be mobilized all able-bodied elements from the parasitic and intermediary classes of the population, can be capable of reconstructing the whole economic life of the country on new foundations. And this process of fundamental economic reconstruction will develop only to the extent that the importance of political organizations declines while that of economic organizations of producers grows, organizations which can remove the useless political forms of human existence.

The social revolution, which the Russian urban and rural proletariat is working hand in hand to carry out, will be anti-statist in its methods of struggle, Syndicalist in its economic content and federalist in its political tasks. Its triumph will thus herald the creation of a social system that will naturally and relatively painlessly evolve in the direction of the full realization of the Anarchist-Communist ideal.

Closely related to the Anarcho-Syndicalist conception of the content and tasks of the Russian Revolution is our position on the question of the war. A durable peace among nations cannot be established from above by the imperialist governments. It can only be the result of a victorious uprising of the proletariat of all the belligerent countries, which will make an end to the predatory competition of the capitalists and prepare the way for the unity of free peoples. Thus the continuation and deepening of the revolution in Russia – its transformation into a social revolution – is a factor of enormous *international* significance. An 'offensive', allegedly launched with the aim of liberation, can only benefit the capitalists of both sides, who are interested in a 'victorious' conclusion of the war. It cannot benefit the people, who everywhere yearn for a cessation of warfare for all time as well as for the overthrow of the capitalist yoke. The Anarcho-Syndicalists, now as well as before the overthrow of the autocracy, are well aware that 'the main enemy is within your own country', and that the   71 slogan of domestic peace is equivalent to a surrender to the counter-revolution of all the gains won by the people. Only through the continuation and deepening of the Russian Revolution can the conditions be created for the kind of peace that will foster a revolutionary outbreak among the proletarian masses of Germany. Those proletarian masses are already freeing themselves from the noxious influence of the Social Imperialists, who have been throwing the revolutionary internationalists in prison and subjecting them to every other form of persecution. Only the final triumph of the Russian Revolution will make possible an international revolution, and only the success of the international revolution can in turn secure the new social order in Russia.

The forms and nature of the activity undertaken by the Anarcho-Syndicalists in Russia flow logically from their conception of the content and tasks of the Russian Revolution. The Anarcho-Syndicalists do not form a separate political party because they believe that the liberation of the working masses must be the task only of workers' and peasants' non-party organizations. They enter all such organizations and spread propaganda about their philosophy and their ideal of a stateless commune, which in essence merely represents the deepening and systematization of the beliefs and methods of struggle put forward by the working masses themselves. Adopting the position that the basic purpose of any social upheaval must be economic reconstruction, the Anarcho-Syndicalists will apply their energies above all to work in those mass economic organizations which must carry out the reorganization of production and consumption on completely new lines.

'Deklaratsiia Petrogradskogo Soiuza Anarkho-
Sindikalistskoi Propagandy', *Golos Truda* (Petrograd),
11 August 1917, p. 1, adopted on 4 June 1917.

13 *On Trade Unions and Factory Committees* G. P. MAKSIMOV

Until now, despite four months of energetic organizational work, the proletariat has not yet made clear which functions must fall to the trade unions, which to the factory committees, and which to other organizations of the working class. Although the trade unions have existed since before the revolution and have well-defined functions and a well-defined range of activity, the revolution has called into being new forms of workers' organization and lumped their functions together in one heap. Factory committees have appeared, the question has arisen of organizing labour exchanges, and now, under life's mounting pressures, yet another new organization is projected in the form of control commissions, which will inevitably emerge in the near future. Thus the question naturally arises as

Gregory Maksimov and his wife Olga, 1925.

to what relations should exist among these forms of labour organization. Must they carry on the same work, operating parallel to one another? If so, what result will this parallel work have – positive or negative? Which of the present forms merits preference over the others in the task of organizing the proletariat and in its struggle for a better future? Or are they all of equal worth, so that the question of preference need not even be raised?

Political parties, above all the Social Democrats, have taken an active part in organizing the trade unions. As a result of this close cooperation between the unions and the parties, the unions have become a kind of affiliate of the parties, [which] have striven and continue to strive to establish a trusteeship over the unions, binding them to their ideas and aspirations. As a result, the unions tend to identify their interests with the interests of the parties. Indeed, the influence of the parties on the unions is so strong that the unions merely imitate the parties, without attempting to create something new of their own.

The factory committees, by contrast, are the product of the creativity of the working masses. In the short time of their existence, the factory committees have already played an enormous role in the organization of the workers and in the struggle against capitalism. In the future they may even play the decisive role in the final engagement between labour and capital. It is difficult to say at this point whether these two forms of workers' organization will be able to coexist in peace: the one being revolutionary, militant, bold, energetic and powerful owing to its youth; the other older, cautious, inclined towards compromise, complacent, calling itself militant but in reality striving for class 'harmony'.

Several speakers at conferences have declared that the weakness of the factory committees lies in their pursuit of narrow, local interests. But such strictures do not merit serious attention, and at the conferences they

73

received a heated rebuttal from the workers. The factory committees must be the organizations to deal a mortal blow to the reign of capitalism. Control must belong to the workers and not to the state. In everyday life, the factory committees are militant economic organizations guiding the life of the enterprises and the course of production. In the factory committee there must reign a revolutionary spirit which will not allow any cooperation with the employers. The factory committees, in a word, must build the road towards future socialist production, yet without forgetting the needs of the present.

One of these two forms of workers' organization must gain supremacy over the other, and the subordinate role, it seems to me, must fall to the trade unions.

G. P. Maksimov, 'O professional' nykh soiuzakh i
zavodskikh komitetakh', *Golos Truda*, 11 August 1917,
p. 4, abridged.

By no means all anarchists were supporters of workers' control in the limited sense of overseeing or checking. For most Anarchist-Communists, such as the author of Document 15, control was only a half-way measure, a timid compromise with the existing order. Instead they clamoured for the removal of bourgeois managers and the outright expropriation of the factories, mines, ports and railways by the workers on the spot. So long as the capitalist framework survived, argued the veteran Anarchist-Communist leader Apollon Karelin (Document 14), the worker would remain a worker and the boss would remain the boss. A rise in pay, a reduction in working hours, a token role in management – none of this could alter the fundamental master/slave relationship or eliminate the evil of wage slavery.

According to Karelin, moreover, the Syndicalists relied too heavily on skilled labour to carry through the social revolution, and neglected the outcasts and drifters of urban society. Others criticized the Syndicalists, as they had criticized the Marxists, for their preoccupation with the proletariat to the detriment of the peasantry and its needs. By themselves, they maintained, the workers could not carry out the revolution, nor could the factory committees become the sole nuclei of the anarchist commonwealth. Rather, as Bakunin had taught, the social revolution had to be a true revolt of the masses, waged by all the oppressed elements of society – including the Lumpenproletariat *and vagrants, the unskilled and unemployed – rather than by the organized working class alone.*

14 A Note on Syndicalism   *A. A. KARELIN*

Segments of the French workers and of the workers of other countries have discarded the obsolete forms of struggle against the employers. They have changed the organization of their unions and, more important, apart from struggling to improve their lot as hired workers, have set themselves the task of emancipating the workers from capitalism and from state authority. The unions of such workers are called in France syndicates, and their doctrine Syndicalism.

Some elements of their doctrine the Syndicalists have borrowed from the First International. Thus, for instance, they are opposed to the state and consider it essential to obtain what they need exclusively by their own power and by direct action. One often finds among the Syndicalists a strong hostility towards the state as a mortal enemy in the liberation of the working class from the capitalist yoke.

For the Syndicalists the struggle for better working conditions and for the liberation of the workers must be waged by the workers themselves. Self-reliance – this is the watchword of Syndicalism. 'No member of a syndicate can shift to anyone else the burden of his own affairs, whether major or minor.' Such is the slogan of the Syndicalists. 'We need no outside assistance but will save ourselves,' declare these workers. They are agreed that the liberation of the workers must be the task of the workers themselves, 'and not', they hasten to add, 'the task of representatives, the task of parliament.'

The syndicates do not join political parties, although their members may be found in parties. As organizations, the syndicates do not participate in political elections. In their struggle with the bosses the Syndicalists may launch co-ordinated strikes, but they intend to achieve their ultimate aim by a general expropriatory strike, which will merge, as they see it, with the beginning of the social revolution. The goal of the revolutionary syndicates is either the full abolition of the coercive power of the state or its severe reduction, and, in the economic sphere, a communist society for all, the transfer of industry and trade to the workers' unions.

The great error of the Syndicalists, however, is their conviction that the workers' unions need not embrace the whole proletariat, but that to attain their objective it is enough to organize the more conscious and energetic workers. An even greater error lies in the belief of many Syndicalists that the union, through its overall activities, will attain a socialist or communist society. It is completely untrue that by achieving control over production in a bourgeois state, shortening the working day, raising wages, ousting a given supervisor, removing strike-breakers or compelling the boss to hire only union members the syndicates will have thereby carried out a series of partial expropriations of managerial powers that will lead to the great expropriation.

One cannot doubt that the struggle for higher wages and a shorter working day is desirable in itself. But it is far from being a struggle for the emancipation of the working class. Whether or not wages are increased, whether the hired labourer works eleven or ten or nine hours, the boss will remain the boss and the worker a worker. Such a struggle is waged within the existing framework of capitalist society and can hardly destroy it. The union cannot carry out partial expropriations. On the contrary, for all its efforts to improve the workers' situation, it will remain separated from the expropriation of the means of production by an unbridgeable gulf.

A. A. Karelin, 'Zametka o sindikalizme', *Burevestnik* (Petrograd), 28 November 1917, pp. 2–3, abridged.

15 To the Worker   Ia. MASALSKY

Worker!

What were you under Nicholas the Bloody? You were a slave. You were locked up in sweltering workshops as in a prison. For a few pitiful copecks you gave your labour – not gave but were forced to give – so that the fat, ugly, detestable manufacturer, who himself did nothing, could enjoy all the good things of life and satisfy his animal lusts in wild drunken orgies. He compelled you to work so that he, the capitalist, your eternal enemy, could gleefully squander on wild orgies what you yourself made with your sweat and blood, your dreamless, cheerless nights, your slave labour.

That is what you toiled for, worker! So that you would not die of hunger. Nor were you alone. You had a wife and children. Yet what you earned was not enough for yourself or your family. In order to have even the bare necessities, your wife too had to go to work for the manufacturer. She had to go to work to help you, so that you wouldn't go to the grave before your time, so that your children would not be left as homeless orphans to wander the streets.

But even that was not enough, worker! The capitalist fleecer paid you and your wife only enough to keep you from starving to death. But there was not enough for your children, so you had to take your ten-year-old son and put him to work too, in order to earn a piece of bread.

And what has all this brought you, worker? Your life was gradually broken by exhaustion, excessive toil, lack of nourishment, poverty. You lost your strength, grew weak and decrepit before your time. Your wife, who for a wretched existence gave the capitalist fleecer her youthful, bright energy, like yourself became bent and withered, ill with consumption, awaiting only the final hour. Your children grew up in poverty and deprivation, never knowing the pure joys and happiness of childhood. They went into the streets barefoot and half-dressed. And he who overtaxed your health, who poisoned you with the foul air of the workshop for the sake of a senseless and depraved life for himself, who tortured your wife with heavy labour, who deprived your naked young ones of the pleasures of childhood – he is fat and sated, drinks costly wines and keeps debauched

mistresses – all at your expense.

You were a martyr, worker. And for all your suffering you were promised the Kingdom of God. What a wicked farce! What utter baseness on the part of the government and its loyal lying servants, the priests! There were moments when you awakened from the burdensome dream that smothered you, when you rose and wanted to spread your powerful wings, tied fast by capitalism, and fly to the Kingdom of Liberty, Brotherhood, Equality and Love. But even this awakening ended in torment. The hangmen of the people, the loyal henchmen of the tsar, bombarded you with a hail of lead. Covered with blood, you fell and sank again into years of the same long and agonizing nightmare. And the bloody tsar rejoiced and heaped lavish gifts on his servants, the hangmen of the people.[1]

But now the flames of revolution have erupted! The great and glorious flames of revolt, destroying oppression and leading towards liberation. It is you, worker, who raised the proud banner of freedom, the banner of struggle. And day has come. The red flags of rebellion, red as your blood, proudly fly over the crowds. Your gnarled and horny hands have raised over the world the glorious symbol of Freedom.

And the bloody throne of the tsar has crumbled under your powerful blows, worker. Happiness has brightened the faces of all honest persons, who with affection, love and trust now call each other 'comrade'. Only yesterday we were all slaves, but today we are free. The last shots have faded into the distance, having stricken down the loyal servants of the bloodstained, malevolent tsar. The bullets flying overhead have sung their last song to bloody, arbitrary rule. The eerie whistle of bullets has told the whole world that there will march on earth in friendly embrace Justice, Love, Freedom, Equality and Brotherhood.

It would have seemed that, with the fading whistle of the last revolutionary bullets, injustice should have died away. But this has not happened. Injustice still remains in the hearts of men poisoned by the yellow snake of gold, and in the hearts of men who thirst for power. These men, whose eyes are blinded by gold and power, are capable of anything. They are preparing to betray you, worker.

Do you not see this? Then why are you silent, worker? Don't delay, for every minute that you allow to slip by might be fatal. Know this. Know that if you do not take now what you need, what you have earned with your sweat and blood, if you hesitate for a single day, a single hour, you will again become a slave for long, long years. You hang back from the struggle and swallow the soothing tale about nationalization and control. Yet, under cover of this tale, heavy chains are being forged, forged, forged for you.

Look, worker. Already the 'boss of the Russian land' is summoning the Constituent Assembly, elected with your participation, by your blindness

---

[1] The references in this paragraph are to the abortive Revolution of 1905.

and shortsightedness. What will it mean, what will it give you? Men will gather to create a strong authority, which will shape new chains, new fetters and a new whip for you, the 'free' worker. A group of madmen, thirsty for power, will gather there and, side by side with your freedom and reason, will create laws and encircle these laws with thorns, with a hedge of bayonets, and you who so love freedom will become a slave. Again your wishes will be overruled. Again they will put the yoke of law on you, and you, who paid with blood for your hard-won freedom, will again be throttled by the collar of a democratic republic, by the noose of human authority.

Open your eyes at last, worker! You have slept long enough through this incoherent prattle about 'control'. You have not risen in order to guard someone else's property, in order to control production that belongs not to you but to your enemy – the capitalist. Or are you his watchdog? Remember that what they want to make you guard with the appearance of control belongs to you yourself and no one else. Know that as long as you do not take everything in your own hands you will remain, as you have been, in slavery. Only by abolishing private property, only by taking the houses, factories and shops in your own hands, will you escape the oppression of the slave and become the boss – the boss not only over yourself but over all that you have made with your own hands.

Forward then to battle. Forward without stopping, without losing an hour, not a minute. Let your battle-cry be:

All production to the workers!
Down with the compromise of control!
Down with the Constituent Assembly!
Down with all authority!
Down with private property!
Long live the Anarchist Commune, and with it Peace, Liberty, Equality and Brotherhood!

Ia. Masal'skii, 'K rabochemu', *Burevestnik*, 19 December 1917, p. 2.

*View of the Nevsky Prospect, Petrograd, during the July Days of 1917, an
abortive attempt to overthrow the Provisional Government and transfer power to
the soviets (see p. 17).*

Part Four
Social Revolution

For Marxists and anarchists alike, the ultimate goal of the revolution was a stateless society of men and women liberated from the bonds of oppression, a new world in which the free development of each was a condition for the free development of all. The Marxists, however, did not regard the millennium as imminent. They envisioned, rather, an intervening stage of parliamentary democracy (in the case of the Mensheviks) or of proletarian dictatorship (in the case of the Bolsheviks) as a necessary preliminary to the libertarian Utopia. This convinced some impatient rebels (see especially Document 19) that both wings of the Social Democratic party meant to defer the workers' paradise indefinitely, in order to satisfy their own political ambitions.

The anarchists, by contrast, refused to temporize with the state or private property. They poured withering contempt on intermediary historical stages, partial reforms and palliatives or compromises of any sort. The old regime was rotten, they argued, and salvation could be achieved only by destroying it root and branch. Moreover, political revolutions were useless, for they merely exchanged one set of rulers for another without altering the essence of tyranny. Thus the anarchists called for a social revolution, a revolution by the masses themselves that would abolish all political and economic authority and usher in a decentralized society based on the voluntary cooperation of free individuals.

In the aftermath of the February Revolution, groups of anarchist militants 'expropriated' a number of private residences in Petrograd, Moscow and other cities, and used them as dwellings and meeting places. The most important case involved the dacha of P. P. Durnovo, the governor of Moscow during the Revolution of 1905. Anarchists and other left-wing working men seized the villa, located in the radical Vyborg district of Petrograd, and converted it into a 'house of rest' with rooms for reading, discussion and recreation, while the garden served as a communal park and a playground for their children.

The expropriators were left undisturbed until 5 June, when a band of anarchists quartered in the villa made an unsuccessful attempt to seize the printing plant of a middle-class newspaper, Russkaia Volia (Russian Liberty). Two days later the Provisional Government ordered the anarchists to evacuate Durnovo's house. During the crisis numerous meetings were held at which anarchist speakers urged that all orders and decrees – whether from the government or the Petrograd Soviet – be ignored. A typical argument in the street outside the dacha was recorded by

a reporter for the Soviet's organ Izvestia, and is reproduced here in English

Cartoon from Golos Truda (Petrograd, 27 October 1917) by Robert Minor:
'At last I have found the ideal soldier who will keep quiet and carry out
orders without arguing.'

translation as Document 16. Above all it shows the revolutionary intransigence of the anarchists, their refusal to compromise with government or capitalism, and their insistence on carrying the social revolution to its ultimate conclusion.

16 The Durnovo Dacha

8 June. Durnovo's house on the Poliustrovskaya Embankment has become an object of general curiosity. At its latticed fence the curious gather, through its gates armed workers come and go, along its garden paths stroll a stream of people in a holiday mood. Red and black flags are displayed on its walls, while within the garden a continuous meeting is going on. The question under discussion concerns one's attitude towards the present situation. Anarchist speakers favour ignoring all decrees of both the Provisional Government and the Executive Committee of the Soviet. They want to go out in an armed mass to demonstrate in the streets of Petrograd. But other speakers urge the crowd to remain calm and await the decisions of the Congress of Soviets.[1] The latter win the day and the crowd gradually disperses.

In the great half-darkened hall of the palace, representatives of workers' organizations have gathered. Delegates from the factories have been sent to the conference. With great tact and comradely diplomacy the workers' representatives explain to the 'comrade anarchists' the necessity of co-ordinating anarchist activities with the course of action adopted by the whole revolutionary democracy. As a result, it is decided to form a co-ordinating group to link together neighbouring workers' organizations.

In their speeches the anarchist comrades point out that economic considerations have led them to reject the decrees of the Soviet: they have no money, no meeting places for their groups, no means of printing anarchist literature. On top of this a mass of unemployed have joined their movement. Be that as it may, the anarchists have agreed to be guided in their decisions by the will of the revolutionary socialist majority and to notify other organizations of any planned demonstrations.

In the streets and in the garden there are animated discussions. The anarchists, by means of their propaganda, are recruiting supporters:

'We seized the palace because it was the property of a servant of tsarism.'

'And what about *Russkaya Volia*?'

'That's a bourgeois organization. We're against all organizations.'

'Against workers' organizations too?'

'In principle, yes! But right now. . . .'

Someone asks an unanticipated question: 'Comrade, under the socialist order will you also fight the workers' organizations and press?'

[1] The First All-Russian Congress of Soviets (3–24 June 1917) was then in session in the capital.

*The house of P. P. Durnovo in the
Vyborg district of Petrograd, expropriated
by a group of militant anarchists in June
1917.*

'Certainly.'

'You mean even with *Pravda*? You will seize it too?'

After a moment's hesitation, the idea begins to sink in and the speaker
brusquely dismisses it: 'Yes, even with *Pravda*. We'll seize it too if we find
it necessary.'

The audience is stunned.

'Dacha Durnovo', *Izvestiia Petrogradskogo Soveta*, 9 June
1917, p. 11.

*Documents 17 and 18, by two prominent Petrograd anarchists, were written in the
wake of the Kornilov affair, an abortive march on the capital by the supreme
military commander, General Lavr Kornilov, with the aim of curbing the soviets
and checking the disintegration of the army. These two selections and those which
follow reflect the unyielding determination of the anarchists to resist such counter-
revolutionary manoeuvres and to make a clean sweep of the existing order by
means of an immediate social revolution.*

17 Towards the Moment   *I. S. BLEIKHMAN*

*A man may escape misfortunes sent down from heaven, but from those misfortunes
which he brings upon himself there is no salvation.* ORIENTAL PROVERB

The government of the 'salvation' of the revolution has at last saved Russia
and the revolution from the misfortunes of counter-revolution by allowing
the army to fall into the clutches of the Black Hundreds![1] This is what they

[1] Black Hundreds: ultra-reactionary elements which emerged during the
Revolution of 1905. Distinguished by their virulent anti-Semitism and anti-
intellectualism, they launched pogroms against the Jews and attacked students,
liberals and socialists.

call a 'firm policy', 'revitalizing the army', 'the unification of all active forces'. One may doubt that the socialist ministers were unaware of what was going on at that 'hornets' nest', the general staff. Indeed, it was with the approval of the socialist ministers that Kornilov, who on 20–21 April brought cannon to the Palace Square to fire on the workers, was appointed supreme commander.[1] One may doubt that the socialist ministers did not know what the *bourgeoisie* was up to – what its own press had been constantly screaming about, what goals and purposes it had in mind when mobilizing its forces and creating its counter-revolutionary organization.

It is an elementary fact of history and of real life that the interests and aspirations of the capitalists are diametrically opposed to those of the working people, and that for the realization of these aspirations and for the consolidation of their power, wealth and privileges they will use every means of struggle, so that the workers remain completely at their mercy. Nevertheless, the socialist ministers have turned a blind eye to all this and still regard an alliance with the monarchists and the predatory industrial world as the only means of saving the revolution. Apparently there has to be a whole series of stupid errors before these naïve revolutionists will even begin to see the abyss of chaos towards which they are pushing the country. Neither the lessons of history nor their own mistakes can succeed in sobering up these men, who believe that 'historically' the revolution must pass to the generals of a wretched and colourless existence and who have no awareness or understanding of the present historical moment.

The whole road of their 'creative' work is strewn with the bones and debris of absurd experiments. Downright folly, thoughtlessness, irrationality, lifelessness, cowardice, weakness, helplessness, wavering, mediocrity, as well as hypocrisy, perfidy, slander, provocation and betrayal – such are the characteristics of the new 'Provisional' Government.

Absurdity has followed upon absurdity, error upon error, and all the while the popular masses have pursued their own powerful, elemental path, in all its depth and breadth, performing heroic deeds and breaking down all artificial barriers standing in their way. With their great revolutionary energy the masses have long since burst through the party dams, shattering them to smithereens and submerging them beneath their mighty current. They have destroyed all the concepts that were old and stale and refuted yesterday's truths of rigidified Marxism. They have pointed to a completely new path for the renewal of life, the path to which we anarchists have always pointed. They have exposed the ulcers of human existence in

[1] General L. G. Kornilov (1870–1918). As commander of the Petrograd Military District Kornilov was responsible for curbing workers' demonstrations in the capital on 20 and 21 April 1917. He was appointed commander-in-chief of the armed forces on 18 July, and launched his abortive movement at the end of August.

all their gross nakedness and, recognizing the most urgent problems, have advanced towards their resolution. But this popular initiative has been retarded and blunted by the false prophets of socialism, who tell the labouring people that they cannot live without the kulak and his cudgel of authority, and that they must await the decisions of the government – and thus condemn themselves to complete inactivity and to the expectation of their salvation from a quarter whence it cannot come.

Given the friendly attitude of the government towards the apostles of reaction on the one hand, and its ruthless persecution of the anarchist and Bolshevik Left on the other, the reaction has grown and become strong, casting its net over every corner of Russia. Such is the result of the 'wise rule' of the Provisional Government – in actuality a grandiose counter-revolutionary conspiracy headed by the supreme military commander (the 'democratic general', as the Mensheviks and Populists have christened him), General Kornilov. The Provisional Government is quick to label genuine rebels as traitors to the revolution who have betrayed their country by summoning the people to defend it against reaction. Yet the Mensheviks have unanimously decided to support the government, and even the Bol-sheviks have yielded, declaring that they too are ready at this grave moment to support the government.

But we anarchists have a completely different view. As opponents of any authority and any government, we reject the Provisional Government, regarding it not only as a brake on the progressive development of the revolution but as clearly counter-revolutionary. 'Traitors, betrayers,' they cry everywhere. But this is not at all the case. The Kornilov movement is the well-nourished offspring of the Provisional Government. It is an organized campaign of the *bourgeoisie* against the proletariat – the *bour-geoisie* not only of Russia but of the whole world, Germany not excepted. (In this connection the latest advance on Petrograd seems like a repetition of the German action in 1871.) The *bourgeoisie* has not changed its slogans. On the contrary, it has remained faithful to its class interests, defending them to the last and demanding all power to the capitalists. In this respect it has been far more consistent than the socialist ministers.

On the contrary, the traitors are those who have forgotten the com-mandments of the proletarian struggle, who have, by making false promises, worked for the dispersal of the revolution, who have failed to oppose the revival of military courts and the death penalty for soldiers, workers and peasants. The traitors are those who, either from weakness or malice, try to squeeze life into the framework of written programmes, who resort to the dirty and shameful methods – the Cossack whips – of the former Romanov hangmen. The traitors are those who have allowed the dis-arming of the workers' Red Guard, who have failed to denounce the suppression of anarchist and socialist printing presses and the journals of workers' organizations. The betrayers are those who justify murder and the filling of jails with political opponents, who disband the regiments of the revolution, who defend the Hamelin-like policy of the government, under whose canopy the counter-revolution has grown and become strong.

No, we anarchists will not defend this deformity of our times. For a man reaps as he sows. If this had not been allowed to happen now, it would not happen in the future. Russia has already been pushed into the chaos of economic breakdown – the work of incompetent politicians – and a final catastrophe, the day of judgment, is approaching. 'A man may escape misfortunes sent down from heaven, but from those misfortunes which he brings upon himself there is no salvation!'

But the proletariat must not let these lessons pass it by without leaving a trace. It must understand at last that there can be no cooperation with the *bourgeoisie*, no truce or agreement, but only a ruthless war of the workers against their masters. Any cooperation is far more dangerous than a complete break. The futility of the former has been demonstrated by life itself, while the latter no one has yet brought about. No authority, no rulers can give the working people what they do not take themselves. So away with doubts and with hopes in heroes or gods!

We anarchists see the only way out of the catastrophic situation in the following:

The proclaiming of all the country's riches – all the land, water, mines, railways, factories, shops, printing presses – as the property of all the people. The abolition of private property.

The expropriation of all palaces and residences and their declaration as the property of free people's communes.

The abolition of trade and the transfer of all consumer goods into the hands of social organizations of distribution run by members of the communes.

The abolition of all privileges and class inequality, of commercial, mortgage, rent and inheritance laws as the survivals of barbaric customs.

The abolition of all laws and state institutions. The destruction of jails and the liberation of all prisoners.

The abolition of money and the transition to a natural economy.

The recognition of the full independence of all nations and peoples, who must join together in unions or federations only by free agreement.

The immediate organization of the broad production of necessary tools for the people's economy, in exchange for which the provinces will increase the shipment of raw materials needed for production and for the life of the cities.

The proposal of peace to all peoples with a call to direct the present war against their true enemies – the landlords, priests and bankers – and a call to all the oppressed to destroy their states and abolish governments and all their tools of oppression, exploitation and enslavement, so that the individual may put an end to his perpetual bloody nightmare.

The immediate break with governments of all countries and the repudiation of taxes and other obligations.

The realization of these great ideals must be the task of all who yearn for the true liberation of humanity from all forms of oppression by means of social organizations. Only with the realization of these conditions of economic and political equality for all will the earth finally and forever cease to be an arena of madness and senseless suffering, and man, having obtained his full range of independence and self-knowledge, march forward in triumphal procession, ever closer to the reign of light and freedom.

N. Solntsev [I. S. Bleikhman], 'K momentu', *Kommuna* (Kronstadt), September 1917, pp. 2–4.

18 *The Crisis of Power* A. M. SHAPIRO

The last scenes of the first act of the crisis of power are playing themselves out at a feverish pace. And there is only one possible outcome: the removal of the *bourgeoisie* from any interference in the affairs of the working class. This is now the chief condition for achieving basic social changes in the life of the country, the more so as the *bourgeoisie* is marching openly and defiantly hand in hand with the Kornilovs and other plotters against the revolution.

But we must not close our eyes to the approaching second act, when Russia must decide whether to introduce a socialist government, as demanded by the Soviet of Workers' and Peasants' Deputies. If this should happen, the *form* of power would doubtless be different, but the root of evil, the *essence*, would remain the same. For as long as power exists, a tiny circle of men will have in their hands the right to decide the fate of a whole people; and even if these rulers are socialists of the most decent and honourable sort, a clash between them and the people is unavoidable, and their relations after each conflict will grow more and more aggravated and inimical. The new authority will use as much force as the present authority against its enemies, and the struggle for socialism, the struggle for the rights of man, the struggle for liberty, equality and fraternity, will be as fierce as it has been until now.

Anticipating this new crisis of socialist power, we come to the conclusion that there is only one way out: the removal of all government interference in the affairs of the working masses. There must occur a fundamental decentralization of power to the point of its final disappearance as a factor

Alexander Shapiro in 1939.

in the life of the Russian people. The people must not allow themselves to be muzzled again – not even with the muzzle of socialist production – so that they will have to fight once more for the elementary rights of free men.

The transfer of authority to the hands of a Central Executive Committee is not the answer to the crisis of power. It can only slow down the development of this crisis, not solve it. The only way out of the present situation is to transfer the tasks of administration to the hands of local organizations – in other words, complete decentralization and the broadest self-direction of local organizations. In this work the local soviets of workers' and peasants' deputies can and must play an important role in regulating the course of everyday life and guaranteeing the local populace the widest development of freedom.

Only the spread of self-determination and of local self-rule will solve the crisis of power once and for all.

A. M. Shapiro, 'Krizis vlasti', *Golos Truda* (Petrograd), 8 September 1917, p. 1, abridged.

19 Two Anarchist Speeches

Speech of Afinogenov to the Third Conference of Petrograd Factory Committees, 10 September 1917:

If our third conference is not, like the first two, to become empty words, we must stop talking about rights and look only at actual conditions. Political organizations merely toy with the working class. All parties, not excluding the Bolsheviks, entice the workers with the promise of God's reign on earth hundreds of years from now. We don't need laws but specific economic conditions. We need improvement not hundreds of years hence but now – at once. Hail the uprising of the slaves and the equality of income!

Speech of Shatov to the First All-Russian Conference of Factory Committees, 19 October 1917:

The question of the present political situation interests me little. I am convinced that the present political situation, as interpreted by the speakers, is not worth an empty eggshell. Power has been analysed for you from every aspect. But it is simply not true that the revolution is a struggle of parties for power. No, it is an economic struggle. The question is: Who will be boss in Russia? Why are the capitalists strong? Because the factories and shops and all the means of production are in their hands. Who then will possess the tools and the land? If the owner remains the *bourgeoisie*, the workers will remain slaves, even if they get a Republic. The best proof of this is Western Europe, where even with political liberty the workers remain slaves.

What's important is not a reform of government but who will hold the factories and the land. We must organize as a class and not become divided into political parties. And our goal must be the seizure of the means of production. We are wasting a mass of resources in summoning the workers to prepare for the Constituent Assembly, for we are taking them from their jobs to accomplish this end. We must instead send these resources to the factories and to the peasants, and methodically prepare for the transfer of production and the land to our own hands. I repeat: political power can give us nothing.

To end the war it is necessary to deepen the revolution. It's not true that the revolution has lost prestige in Western Europe. We must create economic organizations. We must be prepared so that on the day after the revolution we can set industry in motion and operate it.

Oktiabr'skaia revoliutsiia i fabzavkomy (3 vols., Moscow, 1927–29), II, 23, 165–6.

20 *Marxism and Revolution* GREGORY RAIVA

From the standpoint of Marxism, of 'scientific socialism', the most consistent Marxists are undoubtedly the Menshevik Social Democrats – Plekhanovites, 'defencists', ordinary Mensheviks etc.[1] And it is entirely natural that the Social Democrats, cleaving to the views of Marx, should regard the present Russian Revolution as a bourgeois revolution. It is entirely natural that the Social Democratic Marxists should be constantly striving for a coalition, striving to establish ties with the *bourgeoisie*. For, according to the Marxist programme, the time for a social revolution has

[1] The Plekhanovites (followers of G. V. Plekhanov, a founding father of the Russian Social Democratic movement) and the 'defencists' were Menshevik groups which supported the Allied war effort.

not yet arrived. For the moment the *bourgeoisie* is necessary, and to break with it would be, in the opinion of the Marxists, harmful to the interests of the proletariat.

The chief question confronting the Marxists is whether or not the embryo of a socialist order has already been born. Social Democratic Mensheviks, Plekhanovites and even Bolsheviks answer this question in the negative. At present, they say, this is impossible, for 'the necessary conditions for its realization' are as yet lacking. One of these conditions, in the opinion of Kollontai,[1] is 'the centralization and concentration of production in one hand'.

Again the old song about 'the concentration of capital'! This quotation from one of Kollontai's brochures graphically shows that the Social Democrats, if they adhere strictly to the teachings of their apostle Marx, cannot be revolutionaries but must follow the line of a coalition with the *bourgeoisie* and even assist the *bourgeoisie* in bringing about the quickest possible concentration of capital.

The Bolshevik position on the war, by contrast, is a departure from Marxism. On this question it is the Plekhanovites and not the Bolsheviks who are correct from the Marxist standpoint. If an impartial person were asked to judge this dispute between the Mensheviks and Bolsheviks purely on Marxist terms, then the Mensheviks would unquestionably win, for Marx is without doubt with them.

It stands to reason that the Bolsheviks, as revolutionaries, are dearer and closer to us anarchists. For, in point of fact, their intransigent revolutionary position is due not to their rigid adherence to the teachings of Marx but to the fact that they have shed the scholasticism of their apostle and adopted a revolutionary – that is, an anti-Marxist – point of view. 'Socialism is at present impossible,' cry the Bolsheviks, following in the tracks of the Mensheviks. 'Impossible?' answer the Mensheviks. 'Then according to Marx it is necessary to unite with the propertied elements and to hasten the development of the productive forces, rather than hinder the concentration of production, as would occur under the "dictatorship of the proletariat", the ideal of the Bolsheviks. This, rather, would move us away from the attainment of socialism.'

We rejoice that it is the Bolsheviks and not the Mensheviks who are everywhere on the rise. But we regret that the Bolsheviks have not yet shaken the dust of Marxism from their feet. The Bolsheviks are at the crossroads: Marxism or anarchism? The historical moment through which we are now passing strongly dictates revolutionary methods of struggle, but the effete survivals of Marxism have entwined themselves around the arms and legs of the Bolsheviks, preventing them from getting completely free. Yet partial revolutionism is not enough. What is needed is a clearly

[1] Alexandra Kollontai (1872–1952), well-known feminist and member of the Bolshevik Central Committee in 1917.

defined revolutionary consciousness. And that consciousness the Bolsheviks will find in anarchism. For only anarchism shows that even now we are ready, that a free society is already possible.

G. Raiva, 'Marksizm i revoliutsiia', *Golos Truda*, 29 September 1917, pp. 3–4, abridged.

21 Revolutionary Dead End

The revolution has again blundered into a dead end. In fact it has never for a moment escaped from the dead end into which it blundered at its very first hour, and in which it will remain until the outbreak of a new and genuine revolution. We have already stated many times that, to our great sorrow and disappointment, and to the sorrow and disappointment of many other romantics of revolt, a real revolution in Russia has not yet occurred. A revolution which does not give desperately needed peace to the soldiers and land to the peasants is not a real revolution but merely a caricature. From its very first steps it has been clear that it took a false path, that it is not genuine but spurious and counterfeit.

Just look at where the revolution is now. Where has it disappeared to, this 'political' revolution, not to speak of the economic revolution, which has not even begun? It has expired, evaporated. Instead of altering the roots of the economy or giving the citizens the basic necessities of life, it has become merely the 'revolutionary careerism' of a few individuals. The autocracy of one inept despot and coward has been transformed into the autocracy of another despot, equally cowardly and inept. If the former merited the epithet 'Bloody', then the latter, having perpetrated a new military offensive, merits it no less. The former threw into prison whoever reviled his sacred Highness, while the latter now does the same. One ruled by the grace of God, the other by the grace of 'democracy' – that is, of demagogy.

So what happened? Nothing special. In place of Nicholas the Bloody, Kerensky the Bloody has mounted the throne,[1] and one's spirit utters an involuntary cry of despair and indignation: Unhappy Russia! Have you really escaped from the heel of Nicholas only to fall under the heel of Kerensky? What sort of evil genius has again played such a cruel and treacherous trick on you, that he should change your 'democratic' republic into a new autocracy, the autocracy of an uncrowned brigand?

'Zasluzhennyi proval bol'shevikov', *Anarkhist* (Rostov-on-Don), 22 October 1917, p. 3, abridged.

[1] Alexander Kerensky (1881–1970), prime minister of the Provisional Government.

No revolution of the past has been as magnificent and grandiose as the Russian Revolution of 1917. It has set for itself social tasks and has advanced at a rapid pace towards the social revolution, which will bring full liberation to the oppressed classes – the proletariat and peasantry – from all forms, direct and indirect, of contemporary slavery. Each of us who has looked into the depths of past centuries and seen the strange and bloody liberation movements of those times is struck by the brightness of the present situation and by the level of intellectual development of the oppressed classes. This bright and unique light can be best of all observed in the unfolding Russian Revolution.

Having overturned the old outmoded world of monarchism, the labouring people do not pin their hopes on a bourgeois or democratic republicanism in which 'all private property is inviolable'. We see that the Russian peasant and the Russian worker have gone much further than this. They do not deem it necessary to stop at such limited conquests as 'political freedom, political equality and political fraternity', which one observes in almost every revolution of the past. The futility of this characteristic of past revolutions has been noted by Louise Michel:[1] 'Friends, how wonderful seemed the republic in the cursed days of empire!'

But if we take the soviets of workers', soldiers' and peasants' deputies or the factory committees, which are composed of the left-wing and radical elements in the country, we see that in these organizations the desire for the expropriation of private property, a desire which the labouring people are everywhere trying to make a reality, has gained ascendancy over all conservative or chauvinist tendencies. It is interesting how the yellow capitalist press as well as some socialist papers almost daily cry that 'Russia is on the brink of disaster, Russia will perish from anarchy, from unremitting class struggle!' It is perfectly clear that, from the standpoint of bourgeois state rights and of peculiar bourgeois logic, every struggle of the oppressed for their liberation and for human dignity entails disorder, since the result of such a struggle is the destruction of the bourgeois world and the inauguration of a new, bright and comfortable life for all. We read every day in the bourgeois press that the peasants are seizing the landlords' lands without any payment, are seizing all that they need without waiting for anyone else to bring them happiness at some future time. Nor have the attempts by the workers to seize the factories and other industrial enterprises been few.

All this is plainly the beginning of a social revolution, the beginning of the final struggle for liberation. If the dispossessed classes of Russia, in the course of the present revolution, dissociate themselves from all inter-

---

[1] Louise Michel (1830–1905), French anarchist militant, speaker and writer, and participant in the Paris Commune of 1871.

mediaries and *themselves* take the lead, applying all their strength, knowledge and energy to their own cause, then there can be no doubt that they will realize what they have dreamed of for so many centuries.

The historical lessons of all past uprisings emphatically tell us that what is necessary for the success and triumph of the revolution is the self-reliance and broad creativity of the working class itself. That is the chief basis of the revolution. By setting its hopes on the Constituent Assembly or on the state socialists, the working class will as before remain caught in the web of capitalism, statism and coercive authority, and history will laugh mockingly at it.

Though we cannot agree with J. Mackay[1] that 'reaction reaches its highest point in the triumph of state socialism', we nonetheless say that with the realization of the programme of our orthodox Marxists no one will be able to call himself free, because their subtle form of slavery is not far removed from its present form. All past revolutions were drowned in blood and ended without result because the people abolished one tyrant only to give themselves over to tens and hundreds of new ones – to the deputies, the Dantons, Robespierres and other rulers. We must hope that the Russian people will not follow the same old path and will not rely on Kerensky or Lenin, but rather say to them: 'Get out of the way! Make room for our living and healthy creativity! We want *total* freedom, a higher well-being! We are marching towards stateless socialism!'

Then will dawn the bright rays of Liberty, Equality and Fraternity.

E. Z. Dolinin, 'Chto zhe dal'she?', *Svobodnaia Kommuna* (Petrograd), 2 October 1917, p. 2.

23 Is This The End?

The transfer of 'all power to the soviets' (more accurately, the seizure of political power) – will this be the end? Will this be all? Will this act complete the destructive work of the revolution and open the door to the great socialist construction, to a further creative leap? Will the victory of the 'soviets' – if this becomes a fact – and the new 'organization of power' really be a victory of labour, a victory of organized labour and the beginning of socialist reconstruction? Will this victory and this new 'power' lead the revolution out of its blind alley? Will they open to the revolution and to the mass of humanity new theoretical horizons and break the true path towards constructive work, towards the solution of all the burning questions, needs and interests of the present epoch?

[1] John Henry Mackay (1864–1933), Stirner's biographer and disciple and a leading exponent of Individualist anarchism.

It all depends on what meaning the victors give the word 'power' and the concept of the 'organization of power'. It depends on how victory is used by those in whose hands this so-called 'power' will rest on the morrow of the revolution. If by the word 'power' they mean the transfer to workers' and peasants' organizations (supported by military organizations) of all creative work and the reorganization of life everywhere in local districts so that local organizations are formed and are naturally and freely united, we shall arrive at a new social and economic creativity and lead the revolution towards new horizons of economic equality and genuine freedom. If the slogan 'power to the soviets' does not mean the organization of political centres of authority in local districts, subordinated to overall state political power at the centre – that is, to the Petrograd Soviet; if, rather, after victory the political parties which now seek to attain domination and authority step aside and give place to the free self-organization of labour; if 'power to the soviets' does not in fact become the statist power of a new political party – then and only then shall the new crisis become the last crisis and the start of a new era.

But if by 'power' is meant the organization of strong political centres directed by the overall state political centre in Petrograd; if the 'transfer of power to the soviets' comes in fact to signify the seizure of political authority by a new political party with the aim of guiding reconstruction from above, 'from the centre'; and if this authority is to determine the social, economic and working life of the people and decide all the complicated questions of the present moment, then that new stage of the revolution will hardly be the last.

For us there is no doubt that this 'new power' can in no way satisfy even the most immediate needs and demands of the people, much less begin the task of 'socialist reconstruction'. Nor do we doubt that the masses will soon become disenchanted with this 'new idol' and look for other ways. Then, after a more or less prolonged interruption, the struggle will inevitably be renewed. There will begin a third and last stage of the Russian Revolution, a stage that will in fact make it the Great Revolution. There will begin a struggle between the living forces arising from the creative impulse of the popular masses on the spot, on the one hand, namely the local workers' and peasants' organizations acting directly and independently to bring about the expropriation of the land and of all the means of consumption, production and transportation – organizations thereby advancing towards the independent creation of a truly new life – and the centralist Social Democratic power defending its existence, on the other; a struggle between authority and freedom; a struggle between two long contending social ideals: the Marxist and the anarchist.

Only a total all-embracing victory of the anarchist idea, the idea of statelessness, natural freedom and self-organization of the masses, will signify the true victory of the Great Revolution. We do not believe it possible to make a true social revolution by 'political' means. We do not believe that the task of reconstruction and the solution of the most complex and colossal and diverse problems of our time can begin with a political act, with the seizure of power at the top, at the centre.

We shall live, and we shall see.

'Konets li eto?' (editorial), *Golos Truda*, 20 October 1917, p. 1.

24 Down with Words! *ANNA VLADIMIROVA*

Comrade workers!

When will you leave off writing and passing resolutions? When will this endless stream of words and documents cease at last, which threatens to drown our whole movement in needless and worthless scraps of paper? Newspapers, journals and leaflets are filled with tens and hundreds of loud and scathing resolutions that are not worth a broken copeck. Isn't it time to talk less and act more?

Tell me yourselves – are all your resolutions of much use? Has your situation been improved by resolutions? Have you helped anyone with your resolutions? No, a thousand times no! Are there any among you who really believe that resolutions can get you anywhere? Each of them is as loud as the last; they are as similar as drops of water. These resolutions are beginning to act as chloroform on the working masses, stifling their fighting spirit and smothering the living cause of the revolution.

Enough. It's time to stop this senseless game of words. We must understand that the present order of slavery, an order of violence and repression, cannot be destroyed by the Jericho trumpet-call of resolutions. The walls of capitalism are strong and can be destroyed only when the working class ceases to draft resolutions – resolutions which have little effect on their capitalist masters – and begins to strengthen its class organizations for the earliest possible transfer of the factories and shops to the hands of the proletariat and the land to the disposal of the labouring peasantry.

Down with words! Down with resolutions! Long live the deed! Long live the creative work of the toilers!

Anna Vladimirova, 'Doloi slova!', *Golos Truda*, 29 September 1917, p. 4.

Part Five
The October Insurrection

Apart from the anarchists and some left-wing SRs, the Bolsheviks were the only revolutionary group calling for the immediate overthrow of the Provisional Government. As a result, between February and October many anarchists made common cause with their former rivals. At least four anarchists, for instance, belonged to the Military Revolutionary Committee which, under Trotsky's leadership, engineered the October insurrection. At the same time, however, the anarchists remained implacably opposed to the state in any form, including the 'dictatorship of the proletariat' favoured by their Bolshevik allies. Bakunin's warnings about the Marxists' lust for power lingered in their thoughts. And on the morrow of the October coup, as the following editorials from Golos Truda indicate, they began to fear that, unless the workers and peasants pressed for the dispersal of political authority, the revolution might be betrayed by a new ruling élite in the form of the Bolshevik party. A similar message – that the revolution belonged to the people and not to any party – is expressed in Document 26, written by Nikolai Pavlov, the author of Document 11a on libertarian communes.

25 Two Editorials

We summon the workers of the world to self-organization and self-determination. We call upon the 'former slaves' to liberate themselves by their own hands from their last fetters and to begin to build a truly new life. We appeal to the slaves to reject any new master. We call on them to create their own non-party labour organizations, freely united in the cities, villages, districts and provinces. We call on them to help each other to create a cooperative union of free cities and free villages, and to take all measures necessary for proper work and for the realization of this new labour and new economy, this new and truly human life.

The disputes among the Bolsheviks themselves and popular opposition to a government of 'people's commissars' show better than anything else that 'the seizure of power' and the social revolution are diametrically opposed. The basic position of anarchism is thus confirmed: the action of parties is no substitute for the social revolution. The Bolsheviks – especially Lenin and Trotsky – must in due course either admit this truth, abandon the road

The supreme military commander, General Lavr Georgievich Kornilov, urging
Russian troops to fight against Germany in the summer of 1917. The ensuing
July offensive ended in disaster and finally discredited the Provisional
Government, following which Kornilov, by his abortive march on the capital,
paved the way for the overthrow of the government by his bitterest opponents –
the Bolsheviks, aided by anarchists and other ultra-radical groups.

to power and enter upon the road of stateless communism, or fall back on compromise, that is, turn back the course of the revolution. The seizure of political power inevitably strangles the revolution.

Golos Truda (Petrograd), 3 November 1917, p. 1, abridged; 6 November 1917, p. 1.

26 *Party Blindness*   N. I. PAVLOV

At a moment when the life of the country has reached the brink of total destruction owing to the slaughter of peoples and all its consequences; when suffering, tormented, mutilated people collapse and perish each day from constant hunger and malnutrition; when, seeking to escape from this nightmarish situation, the 'rebellious slaves' – workers, peasants, sailors, soldiers – have risen to defend their rights and their lives and have proclaimed the slogan 'all power to the local soviets' – at this moment we see how the 'party men', that is, the members of the Socialist Revolutionary and Social Democratic political parties, defencists and other factions, because of their narrow party egotism, betray themselves by their blindness and condemn the Russian Revolution to be torn to pieces by the counter-revolution of the *bourgeoisie*.

In the eyes of the workers and peasants the illusion of 'peaceful' social gains has receded into the realm of betrayal. The toilers are standing on their own feet and by a decisive armed struggle will attain their emancipation. And this is entirely understandable, because the coalition government which has held power for eight months, like any other government, can do absolutely nothing for the people and for the revolution.

In the first days of the October Revolution the two-faced party Januses, the Right SRs and the Menshevik defencists, fell silent. But after a few days had passed and they felt that the ground was slipping from under their feet, that the masses had broken with them once and for all, they began their infamous, slanderous propaganda to the effect that the Bolsheviks were acting for the money of Kaiser Wilhelm. The Menshevik Internationalists have also adopted a very strange position. They too, forgetting the revolution, have been egotistically baiting the Bolsheviks.

Let all these party men know that the popular uprising has in fact been carried out not by the political parties, by the 'Bolsheviks' or 'Mensheviks', but by the impoverished masses against the wealthy capitalists and rulers, against the Kerenskys, Kaledins,[1] Kornilovs, and the oppressors of the people in general. It is shameful that in these days of rebellion an honest

[1] General A. M. Kaledin (1861–1918), commander of the Don Cossack army who, like Kerensky and Kornilov, sought to unseat the Bolsheviks after the October Revolution.

revolutionary should, for the sake of his egotistical party goals, resort to slander. His place, rather, is where there is poverty, where the toiling class has risen against capitalism and the state.

What is taking place now is not a 'rising of the Bolsheviks' but a rising of all the labouring masses. The Bolsheviks are not so very numerous, and it is not really their affair. A large percentage of the rebels are absolutely non-party workers, peasants and soldiers. It will not do for the SRs and Mensheviks to be indignant with the Bolsheviks, for the revolution is made not by parties but by the masses themselves, and the dominant role, when all is said and done, is not played by any party. For all political parties are without exception waging a struggle for the seizure of power, and the masses will sooner or later recognize this.

No party slogans – neither SR nor Menshevik nor Bolshevik – can save the country from its present condition of ruin. Neither the Chernovs[1] nor the Lenins, by their decrees, laws, edicts, and authority, can help starving Russia. The only way out (and the masses are beginning to understand this) is for the peasants themselves, in an organized manner, to take all the land and grain and by their common effort begin to construct a new agricultural economy; and for the factory workers, without relying on any 'control over production' (mere control will not solve the plight of the workers, for while the workers exercise control the profits will remain in the pockets of the capitalists), to take all production in their own hands and, in an organized manner, begin to construct a new system of production that will meet the needs of the countryside and of the whole population of Russia. Despite the difficulty involved, it is possible to accomplish this. As to *how* to accomplish this, we have already spoken and will continue to speak in the pages of *Golos Truda*. In conclusion we say: Away with all party debates and controversies! To the devil with party squabbles! Long live the united working class organized in a mighty united army.

Long live the unfolding social revolution!

Down with the squabbling of political parties!

Down with the Constituent Assembly, where parties will again bicker over 'viewpoints', 'programmes', 'slogans' – over power!

Long live the soviets in local regions, reorganized on new, truly revolutionary, working-class and non-party lines!

N.I. Pavlov, 'Partiinaia slepota', *Golos Truda*, 18 November 1917, p. 4.

As opponents of all government, the anarchists rejected representative democracy as vehemently as proletarian dictatorship. Parliament, they insisted, was a nest of fraud and compromise, an instrument of the middle classes to dominate the workers

---

[1] V.M. Chernov (1873–1952), leader of the Socialist Revolutionary party and minister of agriculture in the Provisional Government.

and peasants. Moreover, the vote was merely a device to prevent the individual from governing himself. Thus, unlike any other revolutionary group, they openly denounced the impending Constituent Assembly and demanded its liquidation (Documents 27 and 28). It seems fitting, then, that an anarchist – a Kronstadt sailor named Zhelezniakov – should have led the detachment that, on Lenin's orders, dispersed the Assembly in January 1918, ending its life of a single day.

27 Speech on the Constituent Assembly

Address of Renev to the Fourth Conference of Petrograd Factory Committees, 10 October 1917:

The Constituent Assembly is still one of the illusions we must get rid of. If the workers expect all good things to come from the Constituent Assembly and put all their hopes in it they will still remain under the old conditions. The Constituent Assembly will be filled with capitalists and the intelligentsia. What's more, the intellectuals can in no way represent the interests of the workers. They know how to twist us around their fingers, and they will betray our interests. Look over all the lists of candidates to the Constituent Assembly. You'll find scarcely a worker there. There is nothing there for us. We must win our victories through direct combat and remember that the liberation of the workers is the task of the workers themselves.

Oktiabr'skaia revoliutsiia i fabzavkomy (3 vols., Moscow, 1927–29), II, 128.

28 The Bolsheviks and the Constituent Assembly

I. S. BLEIKHMAN

During the course of the Revolution, Bolshevism has undergone a strange metamorphosis. From the first days of the Revolution, and ending with the election of the Constituent Assembly,[1] Bolshevism, under the pressures of life and of anarchism, retreated step by step from its Marxist position. Not so long ago socialists of all hues vied with each other in shouting about the mission of the Constituent Assembly, proclaiming it as a new object of veneration which, once convened, would remove suffering and oppression and solve all the tormenting questions of life. Nor were the Bolsheviks excluded from this. On the very eve of the elections to the Constituent Assembly, at the time of the October Revolution when they achieved a complete victory over the *bourgeoisie*, a complete triumph of the workers'

[1] The Constituent Assembly was elected on 25 November 1917, and met on 5 January 1918.

and peasants' soviets over the capitalists and yellow socialists, they had not yet abandoned the absurd nonsense of compromise with the middle classes. From its very first steps the Bolshevik government found it necessary to proclaim that, come what may, it would summon the Constituent Assembly and that no forces from the Right or the Left could thwart this decision.

But the Comrade Bolsheviks forgot that, besides these forces, there still remained the forces of anarchism and of life itself which nothing could stop, and that they were as powerless before these menacing forces as a child, and would thus retreat step by step. Life has compelled them to repudiate the principle of state centralism. And it will also compel them to repudiate the Constituent Assembly, which the Comrade Bolsheviks even now regard as a temporary necessity that at any moment may be sent to the devil.

Have we anarchists not spoken? Have we not branded the Constituent Assembly as an ill-concealed coalition of compromise with the bloodthirsty predators of capitalism? Have we not exposed it as an outright lie which we must combat with every means? Down with the Constituent Assembly! It is absurd to discourse with monarchists and counter-revolutionaries about land, bread and freedom. In the end the Bolsheviks will arrive at the correct decision. But it is already getting late. Is it necessary to reconsider what life itself has already decided, what the people on the spot have themselves independently resolved? Do you really consider us Utopians because we oppose any compromise? Will you not, under the blows of life's own fist, abandon your half-way position? Comrade Bolsheviks, it is time to throw off the mask of hypocrisy! Enough wavering! One cannot put forward the slogan 'Down with the Constituent Assembly', that ridiculous idol of compromise, while simultaneously celebrating the opening of that infamous institution!

Away with this rubbish! Let the people themselves freely create a new life, bypassing this morass of prejudice where they will again sink into the gloom of reaction and immobility. He lies who says that the decisions of the Constituent Assembly are immutable, that the system it creates is holy. We say that nothing in nature is eternal. Everything changes, everything is subject to endless flux, constantly changing its form, direction and content. Life is endlessly diverse. It carries mankind in its broad irrepressible current for unimagined distances, opening new and vast horizons, with a thousand years passing as quickly and unnoticed as a single hour of the day. What is great today will not be so tomorrow but will become a fleeting mirage in eternity.

No, artificially created forms of human life cannot be eternal. The irrepressible forces of human nature will burst the straitjacket as easily as the explosion of popular discontent has destroyed tsarism, and will give man free rein to live and create, striving towards the unseen shores of life, life without gods, without rulers or ruled, without authority and subjugation, that is, towards Anarchy.

Thus have we written and spoken since the first days, when the Constituent Assembly was only a rumour. And thus we speak now, as the Bolsheviks also speak, but very timidly. We shall fight against the Constituent Assembly, against shameless compromise with those who have till now woven an infamous net of counter-revolution, who are responsible for the shedding of innocent blood, and who terrorize the working people with the nightmare of internecine war.

No, there is only one thing for honest and faithful revolutionaries to do who want to liberate the working people once and for all. That is not to follow the conciliatory tricks of the hidden enemies of the people, but to rise decisively against half-way measures and unmask the lie of the Constituent Assembly, the absurdity of 'control over production', the harm and danger of state centralism, and summon all the oppressed to the Social Revolution.

We haven't the slightest doubt that the hour is not far off when the Bolsheviks will finally abandon their obsolete position and come over and fight alongside the anarchists. In these days of the Great All-Russian Disgrace [the Constituent Assembly], let the black flag of labour be proudly unfurled. Let all the oppressed at a single call mount the barricades for the struggle against the cannibals and man-eaters.

N. Solntsev [I. S. Bleikhman], 'Bol'sheviki i Uchreditel'noe Sobranie', *Burevestnik* (Petrograd), 28 November 1917, p. 1, slightly abridged.

While suspicious of the slogan 'all power to the soviets', most anarchists felt that the soviets might serve a useful purpose as local, non-party bodies of workers and peasants, handling such matters as housing, food distribution, job placement and education. After the Bolshevik seizure of power, however, they began to fear that the soviets might be reduced to vehicles of political authority, to rubber stamps for the new ruling bureaucracy. A clear exposition of their views on this point is the following selection by Gregory Maksimov, author of Document 13 on the trade unions and factory committees.

29 The Soviets of Workers', Soldiers' and Peasants' Deputies

G. P. MAKSIMOV

I Before the 'Second October Revolution' the soviets were political, anarchistic, class organizations mixed with a classless intelligentsia element.

II They served as centres in which the will of the proletariat was crystallized, without compulsion or force but by discussion, by the will of the majority without coercing the will of the minority.

III The acts of the soviets before 24 October 1917 had a revolutionary character, for the soviets had been brought into being by the proletariat spontaneously, by revolutionary means, and with that element of improvisation which springs from the needs of each locality and which entails (a) the revolutionizing of the masses, (b) the development of their activity and self-reliance, and (c) the strengthening of their faith in their own creative powers.

IV At that time the soviets were the best form of political organization that had ever existed, because they afforded the opportunity at any time to recall, re-elect and replace 'deputies' by others who better expressed the will of their constituents, that is, because they permitted the electors to control their elected representatives.

V The soviets were a temporary transitional form between a representative parliamentary system and full popular rule.

Thus the soviets were a revolutionary force, alive, creative, active, alert – in a word, progressive. And the forces defending them were also revolutionary and progressive. Those forces (organizations, institutions, parties, groups, individuals) which stood to the right of the soviets were defenders of the earlier forms of government and of old institutions. They were hostile to the soviets, that is, counter-revolutionary, reactionary. Therefore, when a life-and-death struggle was being waged with these hostile forces we joined ranks temporarily with the soviets as the most revolutionary forces; joined ranks because a defeat for the revolutionary segment of democracy would have meant the defeat of the revolution itself; joined ranks in the provinces because, even though the slogan 'all power to the soviets' did not satisfy us, it was nevertheless more progressive than the demands of right-wing democracy and at least partly fulfilled our demands for the decentralization, dispersal and final elimination of authority and its replacement by autonomous and independent organizational units.

As a result of the above, during the struggle between the two sides, we have stood on the side of the revolutionary forces against the forces of reaction. We have been guided by the slogan 'march apart, strike together'. But this must be our guiding slogan only until such time as those with whom we are striking together become a 'real' force, an actual authority, that is, an element of stagnation, of compulsion – in a word, of reaction. With the forces of revolution this happens immediately after their victory, when their enemies are defeated and annihilated. It happens because the throne on which the vanquished has sat, and on which the victors will now sit, cannot be put at the top of the stairway of social progress but only one step higher than under the former regime. In accordance with the inexorable laws of progress, the moment the revolutionary force becomes a ruling power it loses its revolutionary character, grows stagnant and calls into being a new force that is more revolutionary and progressive. Once the revolutionary force aspires to domination, it becomes stagnant and repressive because it strives to hold on to its power, allowing nothing and no one to limit it. As a result (and here a simple law of physics comes into play: that every action has an equal and opposite reaction) there arises a new dissatisfaction, from which emerges a new force of opposition, more alive, progressive and revolutionary in that it aims to expand the victory where the victors aim only to consolidate it then quiet things down.

This is why the Bolsheviks, before their victory over Menshevism, defencism and opportunism, were a revolutionary force. But they have now become, in keeping with the laws of progress, a force of stagnation, a force seeking to restrain the revolutionary pressures of life, a force striving to squeeze life into the artificial framework of their programme, with the result that they have given rise to a new force, progressive and revolutionary, that will seek to destroy this framework and to widen the sphere of revolutionary activity. Such a force, at the present moment, is anarchism.

Our aid to the Bolsheviks must end at the point where their victory begins. We must open a new front, for we have fulfilled the demands of progress. We will leave the present field of battle. We will go with the Bolsheviks no longer, for their 'constructive' work has begun, directed towards what we have always fought and what is a brake on progress – the strengthening of the state. It is not our cause to strengthen what we have resolved to destroy. We must go to the lower classes to organize the work of the third – and perhaps the last – revolution. And just as we earlier took part in the soviets, we must now, with the transfer of power to their hands, struggle against them as law-making and statist organs. Therefore:

1 The soviets are now organs of power, a legal apparatus on county, district and provincial level.

2 Russia, having recognized a new form of social life, a Republic of (completely autonomous) soviets, has not yet jettisoned as unnecessary baggage the principle of statehood. The state remains, for the soviets are organizations of power, a new type of (class) parliament, each a miniature half-free state at the county, district and provincial level.

3 The soviets are legal, state organs, organs of a modernized representative system, and we know, as Kropotkin has said, that 'every representative system, whether called a parliament, a convention or something else, whether established by the prefects of a Bonaparte or elected by a rebellious people on the basis of the fullest possible liberty, will always seek to widen its powers, increase its authority in every way and suppress the independence of the individual or group by means of the law.'[1]

[1] The quotation comes from 'Representative Government', in Kropotkin's *Paroles d'un révolté* (Paris, 1885), 181–2.

This tendency of representative bodies, I should add, in no way depends on their make-up. Whatever the composition of the soviets, they will surely follow the above path; to turn the soviets from this path is inconceivable. Thus to take part in the soviets with the aim of achieving a majority and guiding their activities in the direction we desire would be to accept parliamentary tactics and to renounce the revolution. It would mean becoming statist anarchists who believe in the power of laws and decrees, having lost their faith in the independence and creativity of the masses. It would mean, finally, that we believe in the liberating force of the state.

No, we must fight, and fight relentlessly, against this existing form of the soviets, because:

1 The soviets have become organs of power in which the misguided proletariat has accepted the forms of law. As a result, the soviets have been transformed from revolutionary organizations into organizations of stagnation, of the domination of the majority over the minority, and obstacles on the road towards the further development of progress and freedom.

2 Their acts are now acts of law which kill the spirit of the revolution and of the revolutionary creativity of the masses, encouraging sluggishness, inertia, complacency and apathy, and fostering a belief not in their own creative powers but in the might of their elected officials: Peter, Ivan, Sidor, Karp and so on.

3 They are not organs linking together autonomous local organizations of workers.

4 They are now organs of political struggle and intrigue among the so-called workers' and socialist parties, and adversely affect the cause of the liberation of the workers.

Thus we must now wage a struggle against the soviets not as forms in general, not as soviets *per se*, but as they are presently constituted. We must work for their conversion from centres of authority and decrees into non-authoritarian centres, regulating and keeping things in order but not suppressing the freedom and independence of local workers' organizations. They must become the centres which link together these autonomous organizations. The struggle for such soviets must be conducted, for the most part, outside the confines of the soviets and among the broad masses. But bearing in mind that not all soviets have the same clearly defined (that is, twisted and authoritarian) character, it is by no means forbidden, at least in some cases, to carry on this struggle inside the soviets. However, the main struggle for the creation of non-authoritarian soviets must be conducted outside the soviets, and it is to this struggle that first priority must be given.

But now that we have a Constituent Assembly, what must we do if this 'lofty gathering', this 'Star Chamber', should go against the soviet organization? If this indeed should happen, then our cause and our duty is that of faithful revolutionaries – to close ranks with the defenders of the soviets and brand the attempt to destroy them as counter-revolutionary. We must cooperate to disperse the forces behind such an attempt as well as the institution in which the attempt originated. If the Constituent Assembly should go against the people's will, if it should show a tendency to deprive the people of their rights, then it will reveal itself as an enemy of the people, and must be treated as such – the Constituent Assembly must be dispersed.

Although the soviets do not completely satisfy the principles of anarchism, they nevertheless stand much closer to the realization of these principles than any other forms. Thus in any future struggle between the soviets and the Constituent Assembly – if such is in the offing – we shall go with the soviets, guided again by the principle of 'strike together'.

G. Lapot' [Maksimov], *Sovety rabochikh, soldatskikh i krest'ianskikh deputatov i nashe k nim otnoshenie* (New York, 1918), reprinted from *Golos Truda*, 22 December 1917, slightly abridged.

The following article by Volin was written in February 1918, while the Bolsheviks were conducting peace negotiations with the Germans at Brest-Litovsk. The anarchists strongly opposed any compromise with German 'imperialism', and called for a guerrilla war to fend off any invasion. Volin's essay, written in a moving, poetic style, is an eloquent statement of their position.

30 The People *VOLIN*

We have arrived at a critical moment, the most critical moment of all, the final moment. And the government hesitates, procrastinates, conducts ridiculous 'negotiations', splits hairs, discusses, and tolerates provocation. It has lost a week and dampened the enthusiasm of the people. And now, when the hour has struck, everything has again fallen on the shoulders of the people.

We say to you: You yourselves, the great people, are again summoned to take the fate of the revolution in your hands. Again the burden of action is on your shoulders. Again you must rely on yourselves alone. You yourselves – and no one else – can save the revolution. So act. And remember, if you win, do not surrender the fruits of this final victory to a new government, which will always betray you and afterwards put the burden of payment on your shoulders. If you win, then after that Great Victory build your own life, free and unrestrained, without authority, without leaders, without parties. Build it in the form of a free union of your free organizations and communes, unions of free cities and villages, of stateless anarchist communes.

Will you win? Yes, yes. This revolution cannot be defeated. Perhaps not today nor tomorrow nor even next week will the trumpets of victory sound. But no one has the power to pull down the banner of revolution which is unfurled over the vast expanse of Russia and which has the sympathy of the revolutionary workers of the West. The whole task is to hold out. To resist. Not to yield. To fight. To wage a relentless partisan war, here, there and everywhere. To advance. Or falling back, to destroy. To torment, to harass, to prey upon the enemy.

The brigands will fall into the abyss. The abyss awaits them. Forward, then, to the revolution! Victory soars above us. We can hear the beating of her wings.

Volin, 'Narod', in his *Revoliutsiia i anarkhizm* (Kharkov, 1919), 126–7, reprinted from *Golos Truda*, 26 February 1918, abridged.

The Russian delegation at Brest-Litovsk. Trotsky is standing second from right.

Part Six
Civil War

The deepening of the Civil War left the anarchists divided over whether to aid the Bolsheviks in their struggle with the Whites. Although as libertarians they found the repressive policies of the Soviet government intolerable, the possibility of a White victory was even more disturbing. Within the anarchist camp a variety of opinion emerged, ranging from resistance to collaboration. In the end, however, a majority gave the Bolsheviks their support, and some even became members of the Communist party. Their intransigent comrades, by contrast, denounced them as 'Soviet anarchists' who had succumbed to the blandishments of power and abandoned the cause of Bakunin and Kropotkin.

The 'Soviet anarchists' played an important role in the Civil War, many risking their lives to defend the Bolshevik regime against its White opponents. A notable example was Bill Shatov (whose speech to the All-Russian Conference of Factory Committees appears in Document 19). Throughout the Civil War Shatov served Lenin's government with the same energy he had displayed as a member of the Military Revolutionary Committee at the time of the Bolshevik insurrection. Frequently criticized by his comrades as a 'Soviet anarchist', he sought to explain his position to Emma Goldman and Alexander ('Sasha') Berkman after their arrival from the United States in 1920. His views are presented in the following selection, along with those of Iuda Roshchin, another prominent 'Soviet anarchist', who, in a speech to a group of Moscow anarchists in 1920, defended the Bolsheviks and hailed their leader as one of the greatest figures of the age.

31 'Soviet Anarchists'

"Now I just want to tell you," he continued earnestly, "that the Communist State in action is exactly what we anarchists have always claimed it would be – a tightly centralized power, still more strengthened by the dangers to the Revolution. Under such conditions one cannot do as one wills. One does not just hop on a train and go, or even ride the bumpers, as I used to in the United States. One needs permission. But don't get the idea that I miss my American 'blessings'. Me for Russia, the Revolution, and its glorious future!" . . . The revolutionary canvas he unrolled before us was of far larger scope than had been painted before by anyone else. It was no longer a few individual figures thrown on the picture, their role and importance

Poster of the Civil War: under the heading 'Wrangel Is Still Alive' a Red soldier strikes at a representation of Generals Wrangel, Kolchak, Denikin and Yudenich trying to seize the Donets Basin. The anarchist partisan leader, Nestor Makhno, played an important part in driving them out.

accentuated by the vast background. Great and small, high and low, stood out in bold relief, imbued with a collective will to hasten the complete triumph of the Revolution. Lenin, Trotsky, Zinoviev, with their small band of inspired comrades, had a tremendous part to play, Bill declared with enthusiastic conviction; but the real power behind them was the awakened revolutionary consciousness of the masses. The peasants had expropriated the masters' land all through the summer of 1917 . . . workers had taken possession of the factories and shops . . . the soldiers had flocked back by the hundred thousands from the warring fronts . . . the Kronstadt sailors had translated their anarchist motto of direct action into the everyday life of the Revolution . . . the Left Socialist Revolutionists, as also the anarchists, had encouraged the peasantry in socializing the land. . . . All these forces had helped to energize the storm that broke all over Russia, finding full expression and release in the terrific sweep of October.

Such was the epic of dazzling beauty and overwhelming power, infused with palpitating life by the ardour and eloquence of our friend. Presently Bill himself broke the spell. He had shown us the transformation in the soul of Russia, he continued; he would have to let us see her ills of the body as well. "Not to prejudice you," he emphasized, "as has been feared by people whose criterion of revolutionary integrity is a membership card." Before long we would ourselves meet the appalling afflictions that were sapping the country's strength, he said. His object was merely to prepare us – to help us diagnose the source of the disease, to point out the danger of its spreading and enable us to see that only the most drastic measures could effect a cure. The Russian experience had taught him that we anarchists had been the romanticists of revolution, forgetful of the cost it would entail, the frightful price the enemies of the Revolution would exact, the fiendish methods they would resort to in order to destroy its gains. One cannot fight fire and sword with only the logic and justice of one's ideal. The counter-revolutionists had combined to isolate and starve Russia, and the blockade was taking a frightful toll of human life. The intervention and the destruction in its wake, the numerous White attacks, costing oceans of blood, the hordes of Denikin, Kolchak and Yudenich;[1] their pogroms, bestial revenge, and the general havoc wrought had imposed on the Revolution a warfare that its most far-sighted exponents had never dreamed about. A warfare not always in keeping with our romantic ideas of revolutionary ethics, indispensable none the less to drive off the hungry wolves ready to tear the Revolution limb from limb. He had not ceased to be an anarchist, Bill assured us; he had not become indifferent to the menace of a Marxian State machine. That danger was no longer a subject for theoretic

[1] Denikin, Kolchak and Yudenich were the principal White commanders of the southern, eastern and western fronts respectively.

discussion, but an actual reality because of the existing bureaucracy, in-efficiency and corruption. He loathed the dictatorship and its handmaiden, the Cheka, with their ruthless suppression of thought, speech and initiative. But it was an unavoidable evil. The anarchists had been the first to respond to Lenin's essentially anarchistic call to revolution. They had the right to demand an accounting. "And we will! Never doubt that," Bill fairly shouted, "we will! But not now, not now! Not while every nerve must be strained to save Russia from the reactionary elements which are desperately fighting to come back to power." He had not joined the Communist Party, and never would, Bill assured us. But he was with the Bolsheviki and he would continue until every front had been liquidated and the last enemy driven to cover, like Yudenich, Denikin, and the rest of the tsarist gang. "And so will you, dear Emma and Sasha," Bill concluded: "I am certain of it."

In the evening I attended the Anarchist Conference at the Club. First *dokladi* were read, reports of activities of an educational and propagandistic character; then speeches were delivered by Anarchists of various schools, all critical of the existing regime. Some were very outspoken, in spite of the presence of several "suspicious ones", Chekists evidently. The Univer-salists, a new, distinctively Russian current, took a Center position, not so fully in accord with the Bolsheviki as the Anarchists of the moderate *Golos Truda* Group, but less antagonistic than the extreme wing. The most interesting talk was an impromptu speech by Roshchin, a popular univer-sity lecturer and old Anarchist. With biting irony he castigated the Left and Center for their lukewarm, almost antagonistic, attitude to the Bolsheviki. He eulogized the revolutionary role of the Communist Party, and called Lenin the greatest man of the age. He dwelt on the historic mission of the Bolsheviki, and asserted that they are directing the Revolution toward the Anarchist society, which will secure full individual liberty and social well-being. "It is the duty of every Anarchist to work whole-heartedly with the Communists, who are the advance guard of the Revolution," he declared. "Leave your theories alone, and do practical work for the reconstruction of Russia. The need is great, and the Bolsheviki welcome you."

"He's a Sovietsky Anarchist," came sarcastically from the audience.

Most of those present resented Roshchin's attitude, but his appeal stirred me. I felt that he suggested the only way, under the circumstances, of aiding the Revolution and preparing the masses for libertarian, non-governmental Communism.

First part: Emma Goldman, *Living My Life* (2 vols., New York, 1931), II, 729–31. Second part: Alexander Berkman, *The Bolshevik Myth* (New York, 1925), 67–8.

During the spring of 1918, local anarchist groups began to form armed detachments of Black Guards which sometimes carried out 'expropriations', that is, held up banks, shops and private homes. Most of their comrades – especially the 'Soviet Anarchists' – condemned such acts as parodies of the libertarian ideal, which wasted precious lives, demoralized the movement's true adherents and discredited anarchism in the eyes of the general public (Document 32).

After the bitter opposition of the anarchists to the treaty of Brest-Litovsk their formation of armed guards and occasional underworld excursions led the Bolsheviks to act against them. On the night of 11–12 April 1918, the Cheka raided twenty-six anarchist centres in Moscow, killing or wounding some forty anarchists and taking more than five hundred prisoners. Anarkhiia (Anarchy), the organ of the Moscow Federation of Anarchists, was temporarily shut down, but its sister journal in Petrograd, Burevestnik (The Stormy Petrel), denounced the Bolsheviks in an editorial reproduced below as Document 33.

32 Declaration on Expropriations

The experience of the Russian Revolution has made it clear to all that so-called 'expropriations' of money for the workers' movement bring only harm and wreck the lives of the best people while attracting the unprincipled and unstable. All without exception recognize the injury which results from the practice of 'expropriation'.

At first there were 'big' expropriations, expropriations of state funds. These became surrounded with an aureole because of the courage and daring with which they were carried out. But life ruthlessly tore away that aureole. Yes, honest revolutionaries sincerely wanted to serve the revolution, but in the inevitable course of events everything became sullied with vulgarity and greed.

After the big state expropriations came big private ones. The enthusiasm was smaller and the vulgarity and pettiness greater. And men perished – sometimes the very best men!

A third variety earned the epithet of 'small' expropriations. What a nightmarish time, how much blood was spilled, what base instincts were aroused! And finally came the last stage of degradation: the dispatch of 'mandates' to private homes with threats in the event of non-payment. What filth and foolishness!

We know that these groups fought with such methods only in hopes of setting things on the right path. But in vain. 'Compulsion can never put things right. It must be abolished,' wrote Proudhon. 'Expropriation' cannot be ennobled. We must emphatically and irrevocably repudiate it in every shape and form.

The opportunity to work is opening up in Russia. And we, the under-signed, declare that we shall fight every attempt to revive expropriation. We shall fight with energy and determination.

Roshchin, Orgeiani, I——va[1]

'Zaiavlenie ob ekspropriatsiiakh', *Golos Anarkhista*
(Ekaterinoslav), 11 March 1918, p. 5.

33 Raids on Anarchists

We have reached the limit! The Bolsheviks have lost their senses. They have betrayed the proletariat and attacked the anarchists. They have joined the Black Hundred generals and the counter-revolutionary *bourgeoisie*. They have declared war on revolutionary anarchism.

The Bolsheviks want to purchase the good will of the *bourgeoisie* with the heads of anarchists. The anarchists did not desire any clash. We regarded you [Bolsheviks] as our revolutionary brothers. But you have proved to be traitors. You are Cains – you have killed your brothers. You are also Judases, betrayers. Lenin has built his November throne on our bones. Now he is resting and arranging for 'breathing spaces' on our dead bodies, the bodies of anarchists. You say the anarchists are suppressed. But this is only your 16–18 July. Our November is still ahead.[2]

There can be no peace with traitors to the working class. The executioners of the revolution wish to become the executioners of anarchism.

Burevestnik (Petrograd), 13 April 1918, p. 1.

The breathing space that Lenin won at Brest-Litovsk was of short duration. By the summer of 1918 the Bolshevik regime was plunged in a life-and-death struggle with its enemies, both foreign and domestic. While most anarchists continued to support the government, a growing number called for a mass rising against Reds and Whites alike (Documents 34–36). Fiery manifestos, such as those in Document 34, encouraged the people to revolt against their new masters. In the south, a spawning ground for anarchist 'battle detachments', the Bakunin Partisans of Ekaterinoslav sang of a new 'era of dynamite' that would eliminate the oppressors of every political hue (Document 35). And in Moscow, the new capital, anarchist Black Guards who had survived the Cheka raids of April 1918 went so far as to

[1] The signatories, all veteran anarchists, are Iuda Roshchin, Georgi Gogelia (pseudonym Orgeiani) and Gogelia's wife, Lydia Ikonnikova.

[2] The expression 'breathing space' was used by Lenin to justify the Brest-Litovsk agreement. 'Our 16–18 July' refers to the abortive July Days of 1917, which were followed three months later by the successful Bolshevik Revolution – Lenin's 'November throne'.

plan an armed seizure of the city, but were talked out of it by their more moderate comrades. The campaign of terrorism continued for many months, reaching a climax in September 1919, when a group of 'underground anarchists', in league with Left SRs, bombed the Moscow headquarters of the Communist party, killing or wounding sixty-seven people. This, however, only led to greater repression, as will be seen in Part Eight on 'Anarchists in Prison'.

34 *Arise People!*   Two Proclamations

ARISE PEOPLE!
THE SOCIAL-VAMPIRES ARE DRINKING YOUR BLOOD!
THOSE WHO EARLIER CRIED OUT FOR LIBERTY, FRATERNITY AND EQUALITY ARE CREATING TERRIBLE VIOLENCE!
THE SHOOTING OF PRISONERS IS OCCURRING NOW WITHOUT TRIAL OR INVESTIGATION AND EVEN WITHOUT THEIR 'REVOLUTIONARY' TRIBUNAL.
THE BOLSHEVIKS HAVE BECOME MONARCHISTS.
PEOPLE! THE GENDARME'S BOOT IS CRUSHING ALL YOUR BEST FEELINGS AND DESIRES.
THERE IS NO FREE SPEECH, NO FREE PRESS, NO FREE HOUSING. EVERYWHERE THERE ARE ONLY BLOOD, MOANS, TEARS AND VIOLENCE.
YOUR ENEMIES SUMMON HUNGER TO HELP THEM IN THEIR STRUGGLE WITH YOU.
ARISE THEN PEOPLE!
DESTROY THE PARASITES WHO TORMENT YOU!
DESTROY ALL WHO OPPRESS YOU!
CREATE YOUR OWN HAPPINESS YOURSELVES. DO NOT TRUST YOUR FATE TO ANYONE.
ARISE PEOPLE! CREATE ANARCHY AND THE COMMUNE!

TERROR, DISCONTENT, HATRED AGAINST EVERYONE AND EVERYTHING.
GROANS OF THE HUNGRY, TEARS OF WIVES, MOTHERS.
PROTESTS AND DESPAIR OF THE ABUSED.
CRIES OF THE SICK AND DYING.
VENGEANCE OF THE WEAK.
THE TRIUMPH OF POVERTY.
REVENGE AND DEFIANCE OF THE INSULTED.
MORE HATE, MORE ANGER AGAINST THIS ENSLAVEMENT!
MAY THIS ODIOUS AND WORTHLESS WORLD ROT!
WORLD OF MASTERS AND SLAVES, WORLD OF ENSLAVERS AND ENSLAVED!

WORLD OF THE SATED AND THE HUNGRY!
AWAY WITH GRIEF AND DEJECTION!
ONWARD TO LIBERTY AND EQUALITY!
PULL DOWN THE WALLS OF THE PRISONS!
BRING FREEDOM TO ALL THE WRETCHED OF THE EARTH!
DESTROY THE CULTURE OF THE OPPRESSORS!
SMASH 'YOUR' EARTHLY AND HEAVENLY IDOLS!
CAST ANGER AND HATE TO THE FLAMES!
TO THE FLAMES WITH LAWS AND RULES SET DOWN BY
'GOD' AND AUTHORITY!
TEAR UP BY THE ROOTS THIS CONTEMPTIBLE WORLD!
AND ON ITS RUINS BUILD A BRIGHT, SORROWLESS
WORLD, WITH FREEDOM, LOVE, EQUALITY AND BROTHER-
HOOD FOR ALL THE PEOPLE!

Vestnik Anarkhii (Briansk), 14 July 1918, p. 1; 24 July
1918, p. 1.

35 *Era of Dynamite*

> Dear to us the legacy of Ravachol
> And the last speech of Henry,[1]
> For the slogan 'Commune and Liberty'
> We are ready to lay down our lives!
>
> Down with the noise of church bells!
> We shall sound a different alarm,
> With explosions and groans in the land
> We shall build our own harmony!

M. N. Chudnov, *Pod chernym znamenem (zapiski
anarkhista)* (Moscow, 1930), 53.

36 *To the Anarchists*   VICTOR TRIUK

> The time has come
> To throw off the yoke
> Of capitalism.
> All fetters,
> Commissars,

[1] Ravachol and Emile Henry were both executed as terrorists during the 'era of
dynamite' in France in the early 1890s.

Generals,
Tribunals,
And priests.
For order
And science
And laws –
What are they?
Invented
From boredom
By great men
In cabinets!
The old world
We'll destroy
And wreck
And burn!
Not 'order'.
We'll build,
Without it
We'll live!
But the great
Commune
To bayonets
Cannot fall!
Before it
On their knees
All will bend,
Even authority!
So quickly
My brothers
Let's raise
The black flag!
And grasp
The hand
Of all
The oppressed!

Viktor Triuk, 'Anarkhistam', *Burevestnik*, 5 March 1918, p. 3.

Throughout the Civil War the anarchists kept up a steady barrage of criticism against the Soviet government. Ever since the October Revolution their grievances had been accumulating: the creation of a central Soviet, the formation of the Cheka, the nationalization of the land, the subjugation of the factory committees – the emergence, in short, of what the anarchists termed a 'commissarocracy'. At the First All-Russian Conference of Anarcho-Syndicalists, which met in Moscow in August 1918, a whole battery of resolutions was adopted condemning the political and economic policies of the Bolsheviks. Three of these resolutions – on the present moment, on the soviets, and on trade unions and factory committees – make up the following selection.

37 Three Resolutions

A ON THE PRESENT MOMENT

Recognizing that our revolution is a social revolution which must ignite the flames of a decisive class conflict throughout the world, and bearing in mind that it is menaced at present by a three-pronged counter-revolution – the foreign *bourgeoisie*; the internal counter-revolution; and the present ruling party, which has become counter-revolutionary owing to the Brest-Litovsk peace and the consequent betrayal of the proletariat and peasantry of Poland, Lithuania, the Ukraine, Finland and elsewhere – the First All-Russian Conference of Anarcho-Syndicalists deems it necessary to organize its forces as quickly as possible for a struggle against the enemies of the working class and of the revolution, and for the revolution's further deepening and continuation.

With this end in view, the Anarcho-Syndicalist Conference recommends to its comrades, at the present moment, to instil in the consciousness of the working masses the necessity of waging a struggle:

1 for emancipation from state capitalism and all authority;

2 for a *communal* revolution in the political sphere through an alliance of free soviets on the basis of federalism, and for a *syndicalist* revolution in the economic sphere through a similar alliance of independent worker and peasant producers' organizations;

3 for the establishment of *free soviets* of workers' and peasants' representatives, and the abolition of the Soviet of People's Commissars as an organization inimical to the interests of the working class;

4 for the abolition of the army as an institution, and for the universal arming of the workers and peasants, exposing as humbug the concept of a 'socialist fatherland', which can only be the entire world;

5 against the black counter-revolutionaries, such as the Czechoslovaks and other hirelings of world imperialism, not forgetting that the once arch-revolutionary Bolshevik party has become a party of stagnation and reaction;

6 for the transfer of the food question to the hands of proletarian and peasant organizations, and for the cessation of armed expeditions[1] into the countryside, which only arouse the peasants against the workers, thereby weakening the revolutionary front and playing into the hands of the counter-revolution.

B ON THE SOVIETS

Bearing in mind:

1 the role of the soviets in the struggle against counter-revolution;

2 that discontent among the workers over Bolshevik tactics in the soviets and other workers' organizations is growing;

3 that the Bolshevik dictatorship over the soviets and workers' organizations is pushing the workers to the right, towards the Constituent Assembly;

4 that to extricate the revolution from this blind alley demands of the toilers great strength, energy and skill in resurrecting the soviets as their own purely class organizations; and

5 that the toilers, for a victorious struggle, must have a clearly defined conception of the soviets;

We Anarcho-Syndicalists declare:

1 that we stand behind the soviets. We are for the soviets which aim to destroy the existing centralist forms.

2 We have fought and will continue to fight for the soviets as *a transitional political form*, for we believe that a federation of free cities and communes is a transitional form of the political organization of society, which must inevitably precede the complete abolition of the state and the final triumph of communism.

3 We are for the soviets but categorically against the Soviet of People's Commissars as an organ which does not stem from the soviet structure but only interferes with its work.

4 We are for effective soviets organized on collective lines with the direct delegation of workers and peasants from every factory, workshop, village, etc., and not political chatterboxes gaining entry through party lists and turning the soviets into talking shops.

5 We are for a federation of soviets in which the local autonomous soviets are united in the districts and the latter in the provinces, and which periodically convenes an All-Russian Congress of Soviets that will divide itself into commissions on the model of the individual soviets.

6 *We are for free soviets*, whose decisions can be arrived at only after dis-

[1] That is, the detachments sent by the Bolsheviks to requisition food from the peasantry.

cussion among their electors in the localities. Therefore the Conference of Anarcho-Syndicalists recommends to its comrades that they enter the local soviets and remain aloof from central committees and party committees of every sort if they aim to conduct free and creative work.

C ON TRADE UNIONS AND FACTORY COMMITTEES

1 The desperate economic situation of the country, brought about by the rapacity and warfare of the imperialist *bourgeoisie*, requires an immediate and fundamental revolution in the area of economic relations. It requires the immediate abolition of the state capitalist system and its replacement by a socialist system on anarchist-communist lines.

2 The workers' organizations must take a most active part in this cause, each in its own defined sphere of life, refusing to allow the slightest interference from the state or any statist organizations whatever.

3 As the unfolding revolution has shown, the trade unions cannot serve as the axis of the labour movement, for they correspond neither in form nor in essence to the changing political and economic situation. What is now needed is a new form of workers' organization, one that fully corresponds in structure as well as in essence to the new revolutionary forms of political and economic life. This – the cherished offspring of the great workers' revolution – is the factory committee. From now on the entire focus of the workers' aspirations must be transferred to these organizational forms.

4 The trade unions, as they are commonly understood, are dead organizations. Henceforth they must become a branch of the factory committees, carrying on completely autonomous work in the following areas:

a cultural and educational (at least wherever proletarian cultural and educational organizations have not yet taken firm root);

b mutual aid;

c the organization of charity.

But the unions must in no way interfere with the work of the factory committees, labour exchanges, or workers' consumer cooperatives.

5 The factory committee is a fighting organizational form of the entire workers' movement, more perfect than the soviet of workers', soldiers' and peasants' deputies in that it is a basic self-governing producers' organization under the continuous and alert control of the workers. On its shoulders the revolution has placed the task of reconstructing economic life along communist lines. In those areas of production where it is not possible to establish factory committees, the trade unions will carry out their functions.

6 The factory committee is our young, fresh, future organization in full flower and strength. The trade union is our bygone, decrepit, outmoded, defunct organization. The factory committee is one of the most perfect forms of labour organization within the framework of the present

crumbling state capitalist order, and the primary social organism in the future anarchist-communist society. All other forms of labour organization must yield before it and become its component parts. With the aid of the factory committees and their industry-wide federations, the working class will destroy both the existing economic slavery and its new form of state capitalism which is falsely labelled 'socialism'.

Vmesto programmy (Berlin, 1922), 11–14.

The theory of a 'new class', although it has only recently won prominence through the writings of Milovan Djilas, has a long pedigree. A century ago Michael Bakunin predicted the formation of a new privileged minority of experts whose superior knowledge would enable them to use the state as an instrument to rule over the workers and peasants. Bakunin, to be sure, believed that intellectuals would play an important role in the revolutionary struggle, but he warned that all too many of them – in particular his Marxist rivals – had an insatiable lust for power. Under the so-called 'dictatorship of the proletariat', he wrote in 1872, there would arise 'a new class, a new hierarchy of genuine or sham savants, and the world will be divided into a dominant minority in the name of science and an immense ignorant majority.'

Following in Bakunin's footsteps there came, around the turn of the century, a Polish radical named Jan Waclaw Machajski, who similarly concluded that the Marxists did not really champion the cause of the manual workers but rather that of a new class of 'mental workers' engendered by the rise of industrialism. Marxism, he maintained, reflected the interests of this new class, which hoped to ride to power on the shoulders of the manual workers. In a so-called socialist society, according to Machajski, private capitalists would merely be replaced by a new aristocracy of administrators, technical specialists and politicians, and the manual labourers would be enslaved anew by a ruling élite whose capital, so to speak, was education.

Nearly two decades later, following the October Revolution, the charge that the Marxists were a caste of self-seeking intellectuals who had betrayed the toiling masses became a favourite theme of criticism among the dissident Left. The anarchists in particular argued that the Bolsheviks were a new ruling class which had inaugurated 'state capitalism' rather than proletarian socialism and had sacrificed the freedom and self-determination of the workers on the altar of centralized authority. Lenin, they said, had simply reintroduced the old system of coercion in new dress.

The next two selections are among the most penetrating critiques in this vein. M. Sergven, the author of the second, is apparently a pseudonym for the prominent Anarcho-Syndicalist Gregory Maksimov. Sergven's analysis of the 'new class' not only follows in the tradition of Bakunin and Machajski, but also anticipates such later critics as Djilas and James Burnham and, most recently, certain spokesmen of the New Left for whom the libertarian socialism of the anarchists has become an attractive alternative to the authoritarian socialism which has triumphed in so many countries around the globe. From the Russian anarchists they have learned that the methods used to make the revolution must affect the nature of society after the revolution, and they therefore insist that social emancipation must be achieved by libertarian rather than authoritarian means.

38 *The State and State Socialists*   A. SOKOLOV

The Social Democrats and other advocates of masters' rather than workers' socialism deem it necessary to preserve the state. In words only, in words unrelated to practical deeds, they agree that in the distant future an anarchist society will be created, that the state will disappear, and that society will no longer be divided into classes. But the advocates of *workers'* socialism – the anarchists – declare that the activities of the state are harmful to the working masses, that the state must be abolished simultaneously with the abolition of private property. In the eyes of the anarchists the state seems no less terrible a robber and exploiter than all the capitalists taken together. . . . If the state is not abolished by the popular masses, there will remain over them a sovereign, an exploiter, an enemy more powerful than the capitalists.

The state socialists consider the state necessary to keep order among the people. In addition, they believe that the state is necessary so that, in a socialist society, so-called organizers of production can take the place of present-day entrepreneurs. These organizers will not receive profits, but they will be allotted special subsidies by their fellow administrators. The Social Democrats are somehow convinced that their future state and future rulers will not exploit the workers, but they provide no evidence for this belief. The reason that the place of the 'organizers' – or present-day entrepreneurs – cannot be occupied by the workers themselves and their unions is that they are for some reason regarded by the master socialists as incapable of conducting the business of producing and distributing goods.

But why can't the workers do without the state, which takes the very shirt off their backs and, together with the capitalists, collects from them the major portion of what they produce? They do not tell us why the working people, once they receive for their own use what they themselves have made and can enjoy a free and human life, should indulge in disorders. Yet it is on this ground that the Social Democrats and other socialists eagerly explain that the people need some stick, some authority, which in Tolstoy's words is tantamount to 'physical violence'. Men can get along perfectly well without laws and decrees in their family and comradely relations, in choosing their clothing, their dwellings, their food, in their everyday acts, in observing hygienic rules, etc., etc. Yet there was a time when slave-holders told their slaves what they had to do in such matters. There was a time when the 'police state' issued laws concerning the clothing that people should wear and the amount of food they should eat for dinner. Men can do very well without the laws of 'police states', yet they nevertheless find themselves under the laws and tutelage of the contemporary state.

All states past and present have been enormously harmful to the toiling population and beneficial only to the oppressors and robbers of every sort. Yet the Social Democrats somehow expect us to believe that their future state – where, as in all other states, a few men will issue orders to the rest – will be beneficial to the workers. We know, however, that the Social Democratic state will be the master at every turn. It will organize production, teach and dress the children, wipe away the widow's tears, feed the hungry, and put the anarchists in prison. It will interfere in everything, rule over everyone, and rule, of course, badly. This state will turn into some sort of miraculous machine which can weave lace and act as judge, manage school affairs and make sausages, build houses and collect taxes, direct the police and cook soup, dig coal and torture men in prison, muster troops and sew clothing. There is no doubt that in the state of the Social Democrats a few men will rule the rest, that is, will oppress them, fleece them and make them miserable.

The Social Democrats assure us that their state will be the administration of things and not of people.[1] But we know that at present men administer men precisely because they administer things – industrial enterprises, estates, houses – things bought with taxes. To the usual activities of the state the Social Democrats will add the administration of various enterprises, and in this way the state will grow stronger and more menacing to its subjects.

·A. Sokolov, 'Gosudarstvo i sotsialisty gosudarstvenniki', *Vestnik Anarkhii*, 14 July 1918, pp. 2–3, abridged.

39 *Paths of Revolution*   M. SERGVEN

Is ours a social revolution? There are some who argue that a social revolution presupposes a 'final and fundamental upheaval', while others prefer to focus their attention on the character and essence of the day-to-day revolutionary movement. But we shall not dispute whether it is the movement or the decisive upheaval that merits the name of revolution. For since the movement is linked with final goals and since both the movement and the upheaval constitute a single uninterrupted process, must we not examine them together when talking about the revolution? In answering this question, however, we must not conclude that, simply because there has not yet been a decisive social transformation, there has therefore been no

[1] The reference here is to a famous prediction of Engels that in the future society 'the government of men will be replaced by the administration of things'.

The new administrators: a meeting to discuss the apportionment of communal work for the economy, 26 March 1919.

social revolution. For in order to call a revolution 'social', it is enough that the movement should merely be striving to bring about this definitive transformation. When the question is put this way there can be no two opinions as to whether or not our revolution is a social revolution.

Yes, our revolution is indeed a social one, for the revolutionary masses are aglow with the destruction of the class system; for a countless series of victories has been won by the workers and peasants under the banner of socialism; for our revolution has been a class war. But is it moving along the path towards socialism?

A 'dictatorship of the proletariat', they call it. But isn't the organization of future socialism to be founded on the liberation of humanity from class distinctions? Within the framework of this dictatorship, however, we can see that the centralization of power has begun to crystallize and grow firm, that the apparatus of the state is being consolidated by the ownership of property and even by an anti-socialist morality. Instead of hundreds of thousands of property owners there is now a single owner served by a whole bureaucratic system and a new 'statized' morality.

The proletariat is gradually being enserfed by the state. The people are being transformed into servants over whom there has risen a new class of administrators – a new class born mainly from the womb of the so-called intelligentsia. Isn't this merely a new class system looming on the revolutionary horizon? Hasn't there occurred merely a regrouping of classes, a regrouping as in previous revolutions when, after the oppressed had evicted the landlords from power, the emergent middle class was able to direct the revolution towards a new class system in which power fell into its own hands?

The resemblance is all too striking. One cannot deny it. And if the elements of class inequality are as yet indistinct, it is only a matter of time before privileges will pass to the administrators. We do not mean to say that this inequality and these privileges are arbitrary, or that the Bolshevik party set out to create a new class system. But we do say that even the best intentions and aspirations must inevitably be smashed against the evils inherent in any system of centralized power. The separation of management from labour, the division between administrators and workers flows logically from centralization. It cannot be otherwise. There are no other words to the song. The song goes thus: management implies responsibility, and can responsibility be compared with ordinary labour? Responsibility demands special rights and advantages. Such is the source of privilege and of the new anti-socialist morality. Thus we are presently moving not towards socialism but towards state capitalism.

Will state capitalism lead us to the gates of socialism? Of this we see not the slightest evidence. Will the new government not contrive 'artificially' to concentrate property in its hands, as is deemed necessary from the Marxist point of view? Will it not complete the class stratification of the country, which capitalism could not accomplish 'naturally'? And will the emergence of a single owner really ease the task of achieving socialism? Arrayed against socialism are – together with thousands of former small and large property holders – thousands of administrators. And if the workers, owing to the division of the population into two hostile classes and to the deepening of class consciousness, should become a powerful revolutionary force, then it is hardly necessary to point out that the class of administrators, wielding the powerful state apparatus, will be a far from weak opponent. The single owner and state capitalism form a new dam before the waves of our social revolution.[1]

We anarchists and Syndicalists – indeed all who believe that the liberation of the workers is the task of the workers themselves – were too poorly organized and too weak to hold the revolution on a straight course towards socialism. It goes without saying that socialism will not fall from the sky, and that only one conception of socialism is not enough. But now, in the

[1] Cf. Bakunin's remarkable prophecy in his *Statehood and Anarchy* (1873): 'According to the theory of Mr. Marx, the people not only must not destroy [the state] but must strengthen it and place it at the complete disposal of their benefactors, guardians and teachers – the leaders of the Communist party, namely Mr. Marx and his friends, who will proceed to liberate [mankind] in their own way. They will concentrate the reins of government in a strong hand, because the ignorant people require an exceedingly firm guardianship; they will establish a single state bank, concentrating in its hands all commercial, industrial, agricultural and even scientific production, and then divide the masses into two armies – industrial and agricultural – under the direct command of state engineers, who will constitute a new privileged scientific-political estate.'

midst of the revolution, we must lay the foundation of socialism and create the organizations of revolutionary struggle and of the economy. The plan of this foundation, in order to conform to the plan of socialist construction, must not be centralist, for, as we have already explained, socialism and centralism are antithetical.

Is it at all possible to conduct the social revolution through a centralized authority? Not even a Solomon could direct the revolutionary struggle or the economy from one centre. And if this is impossible for an intellectual, then it is even more impossible for a worker, who is so little versed in the affairs of state. The worker in a centralized state, alienated from his proper way of life, feels like a fish out of water. What he needs, rather, is an atmosphere in which the functions of management and labour are close together or even merged with each other.

The people made the revolution without orders from any centre. They tore power to shreds and scattered the shreds over the immense revolutionary countryside, thereby confronting power with local self-rule. But that splintered and dispersed power poisoned all the soviets and committees. Dictatorship appeared again in the new garb of Ispolkoms and Sovnarkoms,[1] and the Revolution, not recognizing her, embraced her. Not seeing the enemy, the Revolution was too sure of victory and bit by bit put power in her hands. There was an urgent need for systematic organization and for the co-ordination of activities. The Revolution looked for this but too few elements were aware of the necessity and the possibility of federalist organization. And the Revolution, not finding it, threw itself into the arms of the old tyrant, centralized power, which is squeezing out its life's breath.

We were too disorganized, too weak, and so we have allowed this to happen.

M. Sergven, 'Puti revoliutsii', *Vol'nyi Golos Truda*
(Moscow), 16 September 1918, pp. 1–2.

In 1918, when the Bolshevik regime began to suppress its political opponents, many anarchists from Petrograd and Moscow moved to the Ukraine, a traditional sanctuary for fugitives from government persecution. The largest anarchist organization in the south was the Nabat *(Alarm) Confederation, which by the fall of 1918 had branches in Kharkov, Kiev, Odessa and other large Ukrainian cities. At the First* Nabat *Congress, which met in April 1919, the delegates criticized the Soviet government in bitter terms, but declared that their immediate task was to defend the revolution against the Whites. In the following resolution, they rejected the Red Army as an authoritarian institution and set their hopes on a 'partisan army' emerging spontaneously from the popular masses.*

[1] Executive Committees and Councils of People's Commissars.   125

40 The Red Army

1 The Congress regards the compulsory, regulated, disciplined and centralized Red Army as an inevitable consequence of the authoritarian, political and statist path onto which the 'Communists' have temporarily diverted the revolution. That this would be the fatal consequence of pursuing the political path of revolution is something which the anarchists have always foreseen and predicted.

2 No compulsory army, the Red Army included, can be the genuine and faithful defender of the social revolution. Because of its very nature, every such army must, in the final analysis, become a tool of reactionary forces and thus pose a constant threat to the revolution.

3 The Congress holds that the only real defender of the social revolution can be a partisan (insurgent) army. Moreover, by a partisan army and a partisan war the anarchists do not mean small scattered detachments, isolated from the population and acting at their own risk and peril; by a partisan war the anarchists mean a war conducted by insurgents in conjunction with the broad masses of the population, who are determined to defend their revolution with the support of strong united partisan detachments. Such a war and such an army, by taking the correct revolutionary path made by the living independent masses, will quickly, easily and decisively cope with the internal counter-revolution. The Congress regards the organization of such an insurgent army as a task to be carried out *from below*, by the army itself. The Congress calls particular attention to the fact that the present revolution and the victorious struggle against the counter-revolution in the Ukraine have been accomplished, by and large, by precisely such insurgent forces.

4 With regard to the *external* attack on the social revolution by Western and other imperialist powers, the anarchists have always relied and will continue to rely not on the regular Red Army, not even on an insurgent war, but on the inevitable collapse of imperialism and its armed forces through the unfolding world-wide social revolution.

Bearing in mind the above, the Congress declares:

1 That, while not hostile to the Red Army in itself, it takes the view that anarchists should avoid it and continue their efforts to rouse among the masses those living forces which alone can transfer the revolution to the correct path. Anarchists must bring into being a broad insurrectionary movement, an insurgent army. This is the 'golden reserve' of the social revolution, which alone is able, if necessary, to protect and defend its gains and benefits.

2 If anarchists do join the ranks of the Red Army, the Congress recommends that they conduct among the soldiers tireless revolutionary propaganda in an anarchist spirit, striving to create within the bosom of the army

conscious anarchist groups and to prepare the latter for their impending
role as scouts in the active defence of gains already won as well as in the
future extension of the social revolution.

Rezoliutsii pervogo s'ezda Konfederatsii anarkhistskikh
organizatsii Ukrainy "Nabat" (Buenos Aires, 1923), 17–19.

Cartoon of the 'Insurgent Ukraine', signed 'Pugachev', the name of
the famous eighteenth-century Cossack rebel and forerunner of Makhno.

127

Part Seven
Makhno

As the nucleus of the 'partisan army' called for in the preceding selection, the Nabat Anarchist Confederation looked to the guerrilla band operating in the Ukraine under the command of Nestor Makhno. Makhno was born in 1889 of a poor peasant family in the large Ukrainian village of Gulyai-Polye. In 1906, at the age of seventeen, he joined a local anarchist group but was imprisoned in Moscow for participating in a terrorist attack that claimed the life of a district police officer. In prison he met Peter Arshinov, a young anarchist who taught him the elements of libertarian doctrine and confirmed him in the faith of Bakunin and Kropotkin.

Released from prison after the February Revolution, Makhno returned to his native village and assumed a leading role in community affairs. In August 1917 he recruited a band of armed peasants which played havoc with the local nobility, the Ukrainian nationalists, and the Austrian troops who had occupied the area after the treaty of Brest-Litovsk. The Makhnovists also set about expropriating the estates of neighbouring gentry and distributing the land to the poor peasants. Under Makhno's tutelage anarchistic communes were organized, each with about a dozen households totalling a hundred to three hundred members. Though few of the participants considered themselves anarchists, they operated the communes on the basis of full equality and accepted the Kropotkinian principle of mutual aid as their fundamental tenet. Regional congresses of peasants and workers allotted each commune tools and livestock confiscated from the nobility and as much land as its members were able to cultivate without hiring additional labour.

The next selection is a brief but eloquent manifesto from Makhno to the Ukrainian peasantry, followed by Makhno's own description of the agricultural communes which he himself had played a key part in setting up.

41 Manifesto

Victory or death. This is what confronts the peasants of the Ukraine at the present moment in history. But we shall not all perish. There are too many of us. We are humanity. So we must win – win not so that we may follow the example of past years and hand over our fate to some new master, but to take it in our own hands and conduct our lives according to our own will and our own conception of truth.

P. A. Arshinov, *Istoriia makhnovskogo dvizheniia (1918–1921 gg.)* (Berlin, 1923), 56.

Anarchism in practice. Above, the 'little father', Nestor Ivanovich Makhno, surrounded by his men at his Gulyai-Polye headquarters; below, two of his lieutenants, Fyodor Shchus (left), displaying a colourful composite uniform, and the commander of the Jewish division at Gulyai-Polye, Taranovsky, who later became Makhno's chief of staff.

The months of February and March [1918] were a time for distributing the livestock and equipment seized from the landowners in the autumn of 1917 and for dividing up the landed estates among the volunteers, the peasants and workers organized in agricultural communes. That this was a decisive moment, both in the construction of a new life and in the defence of that construction, was apparent to all the toilers of the district. Former front-line soldiers, under the leadership of the Revolutionary Committee, were occupied with the transfer into a communal fund of all the equipment and livestock from the landlords' estates and from the wealthy smallholders, leaving their owners two pairs of horses, one or two cows (depending on the size of the family), a plough, a seeder, a mower and a pitchfork, while the peasants went into the fields to finish the job of redistributing the land begun the previous autumn. At the same time, some of the peasants and workers, having already organized themselves into rural communes in the autumn, left their villages with their families and occupied the former landlords' estates, ignoring the fact that the Red Guard detachments of the Bolshevik-Left SR bloc had, in accordance with their treaty with the Austrian and German emperors, already evacuated the Ukraine, leaving it to fight with its small revolutionary-military formations an unequal battle against regular Austrian and German units assisted by detachments of the Ukrainian Central Rada. They settled there, nevertheless, losing no time in preparing their forces: part to carry on the spring work in the communes, and part to form battle detachments to defend the revolution and its gains, which the revolutionary toilers, if not everywhere, then in many districts, had won by themselves step by step, thereby setting an example for the whole country.

The agricultural communes were in most cases organized by peasants, though sometimes their composition was a mixture of peasants and work-men. Their organization was based on the equality and solidarity of the members. All members of these communes – both men and women – applied themselves willingly to their tasks, whether in the field or the household. The kitchens and dining rooms were communal. But any members of the commune who wanted to cook separately for themselves and their children, or to take food from the communal kitchen and eat it in their own quarters, met with no objection from the other members of the commune.

Every member of the commune, or even a whole group of members, might arrange matters of food as they thought best, as long as they informed the commune in advance, so that all the members would know about it and could make the necessary preparations in the communal kitchen and store-house. From experience it was necessary for the members of the commune to rise in good time in the morning to tend the oxen, horses, and other animals, and to perform other kinds of work. A member could at any time absent himself from the commune as long as he gave advance notice of this to the comrades with whom he worked most closely on communal tasks, so that the latter could cope with the work during his absence. This was the case during working periods. But during periods of rest (Sunday was considered a day of rest) all members of the commune took it in turns to go off on trips.

The management of each commune was conducted by a general meeting of all its members. After these meetings, each member, having his appointed task, knew what changes to make in it and so on. Only the matter of schooling in the commune was not precisely defined, because the communes did not want to resurrect the old type of school. As a new method they settled on the anarchist school of F. Ferrer[1] (about which reports were frequently read and brochures distributed by the Group of Anarchist-Communists), but not having properly trained people for this they sought through the Group of Anarchist-Communists to obtain better educated comrades from the towns and only as a last resort to invite to their communal schools teachers who knew only the traditional methods of instruction.

There were four such agricultural communes within a three- or four-mile radius of Gulyai-Polye. In the whole district, however, there were many. But I shall dwell on these four communes because I myself played a direct part in organizing them. In all of them the first fruitful beginnings took place under my supervision, or, in a few cases, in consultation with me. To one of them, perhaps the largest, I gave my physical labour two days a week, during the spring sowing in the fields behind a plough or seeder, and before and after sowing in domestic work on the plantations or in the machine shop and so on. The remaining four days of the week I worked in Gulyai-Polye in the Group of Anarchist-Communists and in the district Revolutionary Committee. This was demanded of me by members of the group and by all the communes. It was demanded too by the very fact of revolution, which required the grouping and drawing together of revolutionary forces against the counter-revolution advancing from the west in the form of German and Austro-Hungarian monarchist armies and the Ukrainian Central Rada.

In all of the communes there were some peasant anarchists, but the majority of the members were not anarchists. Nevertheless, in their communal life they felt an anarchist solidarity such as manifests itself only in the practical life of ordinary toilers who have not yet tasted the political poison

---

[1] Francisco Ferrer (1859–1909), founder of the Modern School, which fostered a spirit of independence and spontaneity among the pupils. Ferrer, a respected libertarian, was court-martialled and executed in 1909 on charges of plotting against the Spanish king and fomenting rebellion in Barcelona.

of the cities, with their atmosphere of deception and betrayal that smothers even many who call themselves anarchists. Each commune consisted of ten families of peasants and workers, totalling a hundred, two hundred or three hundred members. These communes took as much land as they were able to work with their own labour. Livestock and farm equipment were allotted by decision of the district congresses of land committees.

And so the free toilers of the communes set to work, to the tune of free and joyous songs which reflected the spirit of the revolution and of those fighters who prophesied it and died for it or who lived and remained steadfast in the struggle for its 'higher justice', which must triumph over injustice, grow strong, and become the beacon of human life. They sowed their fields and cultivated their gardens, confident in themselves and in their firm resolve not to allow the return of those who had never laboured on the land but who had owned it by the laws of the state and were seeking to own it again.

The inhabitants of the villages and hamlets bordering on these communes, who were less politically conscious and not yet liberated from their servility to the kulaks, envied the communards and repeatedly expressed the desire to take away all the livestock and equipment that they had obtained from the former landlords and distribute it among themselves. 'Let the free communards buy it back from us,' they would say. But this impulse was severely condemned by an absolute majority of the toilers at their village assemblies and at all the congresses. For the majority of the toiling population saw in the organization of rural communes the healthy germ of a new social life which, as the revolution triumphed and approached its creative climax, would grow and provide a model of a free and communal form of life, if not for the whole country, then at least for the hamlets and villages of our district.

The free communal order was accepted by the inhabitants of our district as the highest form of social justice. For the time being, however, the mass of people did not go over to it, citing as their reasons the advance of the German and Austrian armies, their own lack of organization, and their inability to defend this order against the new 'revolutionary' and counter-revolutionary authorities. For this reason the toiling population of the district limited their real revolutionary activity to supporting in every way those bold spirits among them who had settled on the old estates and organized their personal and economic life on free communal lines.

N. Makhno, 'Sel'sko-khoziaistvennye kommuny', in his
Russkaia revoliutsiia na Ukraine (Paris, 1929), 172–6.

An account of Makhno's military exploits, social experiments, and relations with Reds and Whites has been given in the general introduction to this volume.
Suffice it to add that his movement represented one of the few occasions in which

anarchists were in control of a large territory for an extended period of time. His ultimate intention, according to Emma Goldman, was to establish a libertarian society in a portion of the Ukraine. Interestingly enough, Trotsky once noted that he and Lenin had toyed with the idea of allotting a piece of territory to Makhno for this purpose, but the project foundered when renewed fighting broke out between the anarchist guerrillas and Bolshevik forces in the south. At length, the Insurgent Army was dispersed; Makhno crossed the border into Rumania and made his way to Paris. There he worked in a factory, a fretful and dejected consumptive for whom alcohol was the only escape from the alien world into which he had been flung. He died of tuberculosis in 1934.

During 1919 and 1920 Makhno's Cultural-Educational Section, which included such outstanding figures as Volin, Peter Arshinov and Aaron Baron, issued a stream of leaflets and proclamations outlining the aims of the movement and requesting the Red Army not to interfere. Three of these documents, preserved in the International Institute of Social History at Amsterdam, are translated below.

43 To All Peasants and Workers of the Ukraine

To be transmitted by telegraph, telephone, or post to all villages, townships, districts, and provinces of the Ukraine. To be read in village assemblies, factories, and workshops.

Brother toilers! The Revolutionary Insurgent Army of the Ukraine (Makhnovists) was called into being as a protest against the oppression of workers and peasants by the bourgeois-landlord authorities on one side and the Bolshevik-Communist dictatorship on the other. Setting itself the goal to fight for the complete liberation of the toilers of the Ukraine from the yoke of this or that power and to create a *true soviet socialist order*, the Insurgent Army of Makhnovists has fought persistently on several fronts to achieve these objectives and at the present time to finish the struggle against Denikin's army, liberating district after district from every coercive power and every coercive organization.

Many peasants and workers have raised the question: What will there be now? What is to be done? How shall we respond to the decrees of the evicted authorities? etc. To all such questions the final answer will be given by the All-Ukrainian Workers' and Peasants' Congress, which must meet at once, as soon as the workers and peasants are able to attend it. This congress will discuss and decide all urgent questions concerning worker and peasant life.

In view of the fact that such a congress will soon be convened, the Insurgent Army of Makhnovists deems it necessary to issue the following declaration concerning the questions of worker and peasant life:

1 All decrees of the Denikin (Voluntary) Army are hereby abolished.

Those decrees of the Communist authorities which conflict with the interests of the peasants and workers are likewise abolished.

Note: In this connection, which of the decrees of the Communist authorities are harmful to the toilers must be decided by the toilers themselves in their village assemblies and in the factories and shops.

2 The land of the gentry, the church and other enemies of the toilers with all its livestock and equipment must be transferred to the peasants, who will live on it only by their own labour. The transfer will take place in an organized manner, according to the decisions of peasant assemblies, which must take into account not only their own local interests but also the common interests of the whole oppressed labouring peasantry.

3 The factories, workshops, mines and other means of production are to become the possession of the working class as a whole, which through its trade unions will take all enterprises in its own hands, resume production, and strive to link together the industry of the whole country in a single united organization.

4 It is proposed that all organizations of workers and peasants begin to create free workers' and peasants' soviets. These soviets must consist only of toilers engaged in some form of labour that is necessary for the national economy. Representatives of political organizations have no place in workers' and peasants' soviets, for their participation will transform the latter into soviets of party deputies, which can only bring about the demise of the soviet order.

5 The existence of Chekas, party committees or similar coercive, authoritarian and disciplinarian institutions is impermissible among peasants and workers.

6 Freedom of speech, press, assembly, trade unions and the like is an inalienable right of every worker, and any limitation of this right represents a counter-revolutionary act.

7 State militias, police and armies are hereby abolished. In their place the people will organize their own self-defence units. Self-defence must be organized only by workers and peasants.

8 The workers' and peasants' soviets, the self-defence units of the workers and peasants, and the individual peasant and worker must not allow any counter-revolutionary manifestations by the *bourgeoisie* or military officers. Nor must they allow the emergence of banditry. Anyone convicted of counter-revolutionary acts or of banditry will be shot on the spot.

9 Soviet and Ukrainian money must be accepted along with all other kinds of money. Violators of this rule will be subject to revolutionary punishment.

10 The exchange of goods and products, until taken over by workers' and peasants' organizations, will remain free. But at the same time it is

proposed that the exchange of products take place for the most part *between toilers*.

11 All individuals who attempt to hinder the distribution of this declaration will be regarded as counter-revolutionaries.

MILITARY REVOLUTIONARY COUNCIL AND COMMAND STAFF OF THE REVOLUTIONARY INSURGENT ARMY OF THE UKRAINE (MAKHNOVISTS)
7 January 1920

'Proclamations of the Machno Movement, 1920',
International Review of Social History, XIII (1968), Part 2,
252–4, in Russian.

44 *Who Are the Makhnovists and What Are They Fighting For?*

1 The Makhnovists are peasants and workers who rose as early as 1918 against the tyranny of the German-Magyar, Austrian and Hetmanite[1] bourgeois power in the Ukraine. The Makhnovists are those toilers who raised the banner of combat against the rule of Denikin and all other forms of oppression, violence and lies, whatever their origin. The Makhnovists are those very toilers by whose labour the *bourgeoisie* in general, and now the Soviet *bourgeoisie* in particular, grew wealthy, fat and powerful.

2 WHY DO WE CALL OURSELVES MAKHNOVISTS? Because for the first time during the darkest days of reaction in the Ukraine we saw in our ranks a faithful friend and leader, MAKHNO, whose voice of protest against all oppression of the toilers rang out through the whole Ukraine, calling for a struggle against all the tyrants, marauders and political charlatans who were bent on deceiving us, Makhno who now marches with us steadfastly in our common ranks towards the final goal, the emancipation of the toilers from all forms of oppression.

3 WHAT DO WE MEAN BY EMANCIPATION? The overthrow of the monarchist, coalition, republican and Social-Democratic Communist-Bolshevik party governments, which must give place to a free and independent soviet order of toilers, without rulers and their arbitrary laws. For the true soviet order is not the rule of the Social-Democratic Communist-Bolsheviks which now calls itself the soviet power, but a higher form of anti-authoritarian and anti-statist socialism, manifesting itself in the organization of a free, happy and independent structure for the social life of the toilers, in which all individual toilers as well as society as a whole can build by themselves their happiness and well-being according to the principles of solidarity, friendship and equality.

4 HOW DO THE MAKHNOVISTS UNDERSTAND THE SOVIET

[1] The forces of Hetman Skoropadsky, Ukrainian puppet of the Austrian occupying army.

SYSTEM? The toilers themselves must freely choose their soviets, which will carry out the will and desires of the toilers – that is, *administrative* soviets, not state soviets. The land, factories, mills, mines, railways and other popular riches must belong to the toilers who work in them, that is, they must be socialized.

5 BY WHAT ROAD CAN THE AIMS OF THE MAKHNOVISTS BE REALIZED? An uncompromising revolution and a direct struggle with all arbitrariness, lies and oppression, whatever their source; a struggle to the death, a struggle for free speech and for the righteous cause, a struggle with weapons in hand. Only through the abolition of all rulers, through the destruction of the whole foundation of their lies, in state as well as political and economic affairs, only through the destruction of the state by means of a social revolution can we attain a genuine worker-peasant soviet order and arrive at SOCIALISM.

CULTURAL-EDUCATIONAL SECTION OF THE INSURGENT ARMY (MAKHNOVISTS)
27 April 1920

International Review of Social History, XIII, Part 2, 258–9, in Russian.

45 Pause! Read! Consider!

Comrade Red Army man! You have been sent by your commissar and commander to capture the insurgent Makhnovists. On orders from your leaders you will destroy peaceful villages, search out, arrest, and kill folk whom you do not know, folk who they tell you are enemies of the people. They tell you that the Makhnovists are bandits and counter-revolutionaries. They tell you, order you, do not ask you, but send you, and as a humble slave of your leaders you go to capture and kill. Whom? Why? For what? Think it over, comrade Red Army man! Think it over, you toiling peasant and worker, taken by force into the cabal of the new bosses who claim the proud title of workers' and peasants' power.

We revolutionary insurgents and Makhnovists are also peasants and workers, just like our brothers, the Red Army men. We rose against tyranny and oppression. We are fighting for a better and brighter life. Our immediate goal is the achievement of a stateless toilers' community without parasites and without commissar-bureaucrats. Our immediate aim is the establishment of a free soviet order without the power of the Bolsheviks, without the compulsion of any party. For this the Bolshevik-Communist government sends punitive expeditions against us. It hastens to make peace with Denikin, with the Polish landlords, and with other White Guard swine so as to suppress more easily the popular movement of revolutionary insurgents rising for the oppressed and against the yoke of all authority.

We do not fear the threats of the White–Red high command. WE WILL ANSWER VIOLENCE WITH VIOLENCE. If need be, we, though only a small handful, will put to flight the divisions of the statist Red Army. For we are freedom-loving revolutionary insurgents, and the cause we defend is a righteous cause.

Comrade! Think it over. Whom are you with and whom against? Don't be a slave – be a man!

INSURGENT MAKHNOVISTS

June 1920

International Review of Social History, XIII, Part 2, 268, in Russian.

Bolshevik poster equating Makhno (on left) with Wrangel, Petliura, Batko Angel (another partisan leader in the Ukraine) and the church as enemies of the state.

Part Eight
Anarchists in Prison

As the Civil War deepened the Bolsheviks grew less and less tolerant of their political opponents, even of those who confined themselves to mere verbal assaults on the government's dictatorial policies. 'Liberty', said Lenin to Alexander Berkman, 'is a luxury not to be permitted at the present stage of development.' After the first Cheka raids of April 1918, Bolshevik harassment of the anarchists mounted sharply, reaching a climax after the bombing of Communist head-quarters in Moscow in September 1919 by a group of anarchists and Left SRs. Between 1919 and 1921 Gregory Maksimov, the author of Document 47, was taken into custody no less than six times, and even such loyal 'Soviet anarchists' as Abba Gordin and Iuda Roshchin were imprisoned for brief periods. To justify the repression, Bolshevik spokesmen argued that, with the survival of the revolution at stake, it was imperative to snuff out opposition from every quarter. At the same time, Lenin and Trotsky insisted that no anarchists were being arrested merely for their beliefs but only for criminal or insurrectionary acts. At any rate, by the end of 1920 the Cheka drag-net had swept the entire country. Leading anarchist periodicals were closed down. New ones sprang up, only to be suppressed after one or two issues. Most anarchist clubs and organizations were forced to shut their doors or to go underground. Makhno's guerrilla movement was crushed. The Nabat Confederation was dispersed and its leaders, including Volin and Aaron Baron, were arrested and sent to prison in Moscow. The final blow was to come after the Kronstadt rebellion, and will be discussed in the following section.

46 A Letter From Prison   *P. MOGILA*

Having come for a few days to Ekaterinoslav from the war front at Gulyai-Polye, I dropped in to the Secretariat of the Anarchist Confedera-tion in order to see a few comrades and also to buy a few issues of the "Nabat". I happened to have come at the time when the place was raided by the militiamen, who arrested the members of the Secretariat. I was taken along with them, the only reason for my arrest being that I was an Anarchist.

There were thirteen of us who were arrested upon orders of the Executive Committee of the Ekaterinoslav Soviet, and we were all treated in the same manner in which political prisoners were treated by the old police of the Tsar. An armed squad took us over to the Commandant of the city of Ekaterinoslav where we were questioned and then led away to the Cheka.

Bolshevik repression. Above, Moisei Uritsky, head of the Petrograd Cheka, in his office at the Tauride Palace. Below, a group of workmen arrested as 'counter-revolutionaries' after a series of strikes are marched along the Nevsky Prospect to be shot, January 1920.

In the latter place we were mocked at and reviled by kids. The kids treated me in a way which no police agent of the old regime would ever permit himself.

After our names had been duly entered, we were led away to some sort of cellar which lacked ventilation. There were twenty of us packed into this dark and damp kennel which is not fit even for a dog. At one o'clock we were given another interrogation and then sent off to prison. Our convoy, an armed squad of two people, were misled to the point of regarding us as the worst scum. *They had been told that we were Petliura officers.*[1]

Now, comrades and fellow soldiers of the irregular army,[2] I will tell you in a few words who I am and what sort of criminal I am. I too am a peasant, a member of the irregular army. Like the other thirteen arrested people I am an Anarchist. Until fourteen years of age I went to school. But already at that time I was seized with the revolutionary spirit. I could not silently look on at the mean, base, criminal, starvation regime of Tsar Nicholas, under which a small handful of fortunate do-nothings enjoyed all the luxuries and blessings of life, and *did not let live others*, the millions of starving unfortunate victims who sweated to death in the mines, factories and fields, and who gave their lives away upon the battlefields for the profits of the few.

At eighteen years I was taken away to the army, where I continuously conducted propaganda against the war waged by capitalists for their own interests. I was persecuted and during the coalition government I was thrown into jail as an agitator. After the October Revolution I worked in the rural Soviet of Sursk-Litovsk, of the province of Ekaterinoslav, and from there I was sent to the convention of Peasant Soviets of the country where I had worked as an honest revolutionary until the occupation of the Ukraine by the Germans and Austrians.

During the period of reaction in the Ukraine I worked tirelessly in the underground organization. I was arrested several times and finally escaped. The last time I worked with comrade Makhno. I will not go into detail as to my underground work: Those who worked underground, especially those who know the work of comrade Makhno, can tell what sort of "counter-revolutionary" I am.

And now I ask you, Commissars: Where were you when the reaction was in full swing here, when the blood of the peasants and workers ran freely, when thousands of them were brutally whipped, tortured and executed? Where were you when violence reigned freely in the Ukraine, when the German-Austrian whip, gun, rod, and bayonet were freely used

---

[1] Semyon Petliura (1877–1926), leader of the Ukrainian nationalist forces during the Civil War.

[2] Makhno's Insurgent Army of the Ukraine.

on the backs of helpless workers and peasants? Where were you when the peasants rose up against the German, Austrian, and Petliura regiments, when entire villages threw themselves almost barehanded against the invaders, thus clearing the way for the free life to come? And who gave you the right to arrest, imprison, and execute the sons of the Ukrainian toiling people, those who were the first to raise the banner of revolt, who took the rifles in their hands, having told themselves: "To live as free men or to die in the struggle" – and then fulfilled those solemn promises, clearing the Ukraine of the counterrevolutionary bands?

Let us have your answer, Commissars! And you, fellow soldiers of the irregular army, who have shed so much blood, who carried upon your shoulders the heavy burden of reaction and counterrevolution, who have left so many graves of the nearest comrades, ask yourselves at last: "In the name of what have we gone through so much suffering? Have we done all this so that when we come home from the front we should be arrested, imprisoned, reviled, and very often executed, and all simply because we do not want to truckle to the self-made authorities, submit to laws made by power-intoxicated bureaucrats who forget to ask themselves: Who conquered freedom and at what price?"

Fellow soldiers, workers, and peasants! If you are in favor of this vile authoritarian rule, if you prefer to stand cruelty, violence, and baseness – then suffer that mockery in silence and die submissively. But if you do not want to stand this violence, if you want to obtain full freedom, economic and political, do not let these acts of violence pass in silence. Protest against them to your comrades. Demand the immediate release of your fellow workers who were arrested on no charges, and demand the release of other comrades who are innocent of any crime. Declare openly that in a free country not a single revolutionist should be subject to arrests and revilement.

P. Mogila, Member of the Makhno Army,
Ekaterinoslav Prison

Guliaipol'skii Nabat, 13 April 1919. English translation in
G. P. Maksimov, *The Guillotine at Work* (Chicago, 1940),
413–15.

47 One Day in the Cheka's Cellar

We are at the very end of the corridor leading to the Cheka dungeon. The key clanged and I was shoved into a tiny cell. Another clang of the key and life was left at the other side. I stood still at the door, staring in bewilderment.

The cell represented a tiny room with one window, set below the level of the ground and latticed with iron bars. The window opened into a court-yard facing some mysterious barns. Along the wall, stretching from the door to the window, were plank-beds from which four pairs of eyes were staring fixedly at me. One of them belonged to a pain-wracked, huddled figure, fixed in a seated position upon the plank-beds. The sight of it sent a shiver through my body. Its head rose at my appearance and then sank back into its former position. The figure was transfixed as it sank into a state of coma.

Seated near this figure closer to the window were two young men, sturdy and heavy. They jumped off the plank-bed with great alacrity: one could easily tell from their bearing and movements that they were army people. At the other side of the stiffened figure, nearer to the door, a priest was seated; his beard was tousled, and his long disheveled hair was unkempt. The two army people approached me and began firing questions at me.

"Why were you arrested?" one of them asked.

"Because I refused to carry out police duties while in the army, having submitted a written declaration to that effect."

"Ah . . ." one of them drawled, "you're in a bad fix. What are you – Menshevik or Socialist Revolutionary?"

"No. I am an Anarchist."

"An-ar-chist!" He drawled out the word in amazement. "Are you people getting arrested too?"

"It looks that way," I answered.

"You say," the second one questioned again, "because you refused. Well, then you are a finished man."

A feeling of hatred at this man welled up within me when I heard him saying that awful thing. But I restrained myself.

"And you?" I asked in turn.

"We? We are also here on charges of a military nature. On some suspicion." The answer was given rather reluctantly. Both broke off the conversation, turning back to the plank-bed.

"And so you believe you will be released soon," one of them asked again sneeringly, climbing onto the plank-bed.

"Yes, I do," I said loudly, but with restrained malice, hardly of course believing my own words.

"Yes, they will release you. They will release your body from your soul," one of them said in a quiet voice but with the studied intent of making himself heard. "From here," he added, this time loudly and with a manifest undertone of malice, "only lucky people ever get out."

I did not answer. Heavy silence enveloped us all. Everyone was sunk in his thoughts. I walked up to the priest. The latter was breathing heavily, while the army people exchanged whispers from time to time. The petrified figure remained in the same position. A feeling of distress was overtaking me. Cheerless thoughts began to harrow my brain. The idea that I might be executed shook my insides; every cell within my body cried out against a senseless death. . . . We are all silent. Darkness fell upon the cell. The sighs of my cellmate became deeper and more distressful. The whispers sink to barely audible tones.

A sudden light floods the cell. The electric lights were turned on. I took a smoke.

"Don't put out your match," one of the army men asks me.

We all smoke, except the immobile figure. I inquire about the latter.

"The investigator told him," one of the army men whispered to me – "we are going to shoot you."

"We are going to shoot you." That phrase resounded within me. "How?" an inner voice kept clamoring within me. How can they do it? Who gave them the right? People sit there, upstairs, and quietly, ruthlessly kill other people. Barbarity! It is impossible, it is criminal, just to be able to say simply: "We are going to shoot you." And the same wretches tell me the same thing: "We will have you shot." But how come. . . . The train of thought breaks off all of a sudden, and here they follow already in a different direction. "And, perhaps, they won't even say it: they will just take me out and have me shot without any warning. They will take me out ostensibly for a hearing and then . . . bang, straight into my neck. And that is the end of me. Of course, this is what will happen. After all, they can't leave us with Denikin; and on the other hand, they surely will not take us along." That is followed by another train of thought. "No, it is impossible. They won't, they can't shoot me, they must release me. I am not a White-Guardist. I am a revolutionist. And who are they, the Bolsheviks?"

I am going through a state of veritable hell. I fling away one cigarette after another.

The petrified figure of the "doomed" man came to life. Slowly, as if he were seriously ill, the "doomed" man climbed down from the plank-bed, knocked at the door, asking to be taken out to the lavatory. He left together with the two army people. Soon they came back. I viewed this man with a certain degree of curiosity. He was a middle-aged man, tall, slender; his face was flat and pale. He halted in the middle of the room and, addressing his companions, he said, seemingly continuing an interrupted conversation: "No, no. Today I will surely be taken out. I was told straight in my face: 'Confess, you will be shot anyway.' Now, I'll have to get my things together. There is little time left now. Night has fallen already."

There was a long pause.

"Eh-h-h-h-ch."

No one answered him. Everyone was taken up with his own thoughts. The "doomed" man began to pick up his belongings, tying them up in a bundle. That being done, he took a long look at them and smiled wryly. And then back he went to his plank-bed, back to his huddled, transfixed posture.

"I feel that today the last balance of my life is going to be drawn," he said forlornly, staring fixedly in the empty space.

No one answered him, not even an echo of his own voice, which died away in the cell. It was distressingly painful; death made itself felt. My temples began to throb violently; the head was burning; the lids grew heavy. Invisible hammers kept pounding beneath the cranium box. Consciousness was splitting away; everything became as if in a fog. A savage cacophony broke loose within me; my thoughts kept whirling frenziedly. I felt an increasing weakness, a growing apathy. My taut nerves began to lose their power to react to internal stimuli: "I too don't want to die. I am young, my life lies ahead of me. I did so little in my life. To die under the muzzle of an automatic, to be killed by a Cheka executionist! No, no. And what for? Who will ever learn about my death? And in which way will my death profit anyone? To die for the common cause, yes – there is nothing terrible about that. But now, to die such a senseless death, of what avail will it be? To fulfil my duty? Ha-ha, duty! What sort of duty? The duty of conscience and honor? No, but this. . . ."

The rumbling of an approaching truck broke the silence. It found its painful echo in the hearts of the cell inmates. The "doomed" man started up, and then let his head sink upon his knees.

"Oh, Lord, save us and have mercy upon us," whispered the priest, crossing himself.

"They are beginning," said one of the army men.

"Beginning what? Who is beginning?" I asked.

"Lie down and sleep; you will rest better for it; you won't be worked up unnecessarily and you will be saved the affliction of many a stinging thought," exhorted the priest.

"But then, what is really starting now?" I kept on asking anxiously.

"Shootings!" was the sharp and spiteful answer. "Many a soul is now trembling with fear and anxiety. Everyone is thinking: will they come after me?"

I don't remember what happened afterwards. Whether I fell asleep or just sank into a state of stupor; I can hardly remember. A violent noise, loud voices, the clanking of keys, bolts, the squeaking of doors – all that woke me up. We all jumped up like startled gazelles. "Whose turn?" everyone questioned anxiously.

"N. N., get your things ready!"

The "doomed" man jumped off hastily, seized the bundle with his belongings and shoved it under his left arm. A deadly pallor spread over his trembling lips, which kept on moving as if in prayer. His hands were shaking. Rapidly and keeping turns, he approached everyone of us and, stretching out his trembling hand, he said with a peculiar intonation:

"Goodbye. . . . I am taken out to be shot."

The doors slammed again and a man's life was blotted out.

"Oh, Lord, remember thy servant in thy kingdom," uttered the priest.

"Away with the soul-wracking and pains," said one of the army men sighing deeply.

A long silence!

"He is dead by now," said the other army man loudly, seemingly continuing his train of thought.

There was no answer. A deep brooding silence reigned in the cell.

Maksimov, *The Guillotine at Work* (Chicago, 1940),
425–31, in English translation, abridged.

Despite his unpopular stand on the war, Kropotkin remained the foremost libertarian theorist and the most venerated figure of the anarchist movement. During the Cheka raids on the anarchist organizations he was not personally molested, but in the summer of 1918 he was compelled to move to the village of Dmitrov, some forty miles north of Moscow. There he spent much of his time writing a history of ethics (which he was never to finish) and receiving a steady stream of visitors, including Volin, Maksimov, Emma Goldman and Berkman.

As the Civil War unfolded Kropotkin was increasingly disturbed by the authoritarian methods of the Soviet government. He bitterly opposed the terrorist practices of the Cheka, notably the taking of hostages, which he denounced in a famous letter to Lenin of 21 December 1920 (Document 48). At the same time, however, he was opposed to Allied intervention in the Civil War, and in an open letter to the workers of the West (Document 49) he urged them to put pressure on their governments to withdraw all troops from Russian soil. Not, he said, that there was nothing to criticize in the Soviet dictatorship. But intervention, he feared, would only make matters worse by alienating the Russian population and strengthening the dictatorial tendencies of the government.

In January 1921 Kropotkin, nearly eighty years old, fell ill with pneumonia, and three weeks later, on 8 February, he died. His funeral was the last time that the black flag of anarchism was paraded through the Russian capital. Tens of thousands braved the bitter cold of the Moscow winter to march in the cortège to his burial place in the Novodevichi Monastery. It was a profoundly moving occasion. As the procession passed the Butyrki prison, the inmates shook the bars on their windows and sang an anarchist hymn to the dead. Emma Goldman, Aaron Baron, Aleksei Borovoi and others spoke at Kropotkin's graveside, and students and workers placed flowers by his tomb. Kropotkin's passing sounded the death knell of Russian anarchism. There remained only the feeble consolation that his repeated warnings against revolutionary dictatorships had been vindicated. As he had noted in his message to the workers of the West, the Bolsheviks had shown how the revolution was not to be made – that is, by authoritarian rather than libertarian methods.

Dear Vladimir Ilyich,

Several employees of the post and telegraph bureau have approached me with a request to bring to your attention their truly desperate situation. As this matter concerns not only the Commissariat of Post and Telegraph but the general condition of life in Russia, I hasten to fulfil their request.

You know, of course, that to live in the Dmitrov district on the two to three thousand rouble salary which these employees receive is *absolutely impossible*. For 2,000 roubles you cannot buy even a bushel of potatoes, and I know this from my own experience. In exchange you are asked for soap and salt, of which there is none. Since the price of flour has risen to 9,000 roubles a pood,[1] even if you manage to find some you cannot buy enough for eight pounds of bread, or enough wheat for five pounds. Without receiving provisions the employees, in a word, are doomed to actual starvation.

Meanwhile, along with such prices, the meagre provisions which the post and telegraph employees have been receiving from the Moscow post and telegraph supply depot (according to the decree of 15 August 1918, eight pounds of flour per employee and five pounds of flour to disabled members of a family) *have not been delivered for two months*. Local food agencies cannot release any of their own supplies, and the appeal of the employees (125 persons in the Dmitrov area) to Moscow remains unanswered. A month ago one of the employees wrote to you personally, but so far has received no answer.

I consider it my duty to testify that the situation of these employees is truly desperate. The majority are *literally starving*. This is written on their faces. Many plan to leave, without knowing where to go. But meanwhile, I dare say, they perform their tasks conscientiously, tasks which they have mastered, so that to lose such workers would in no way be in the interests of local life.

I shall add only that whole categories of other Soviet employees can be found in the same desperate situation.

I must conclude with a few words about the general state of affairs. Living in a great centre, in Moscow, you cannot know the true situation of the country. To learn the truth about existing conditions you must live in the provinces, in close touch with daily life, with its needs and calamities, with the starving – adults and children – and with the scurrying from office to office to secure permission to buy a cheap kerosene lamp, and so on.

What we are now experiencing leads to only one conclusion. We must hurry on with the transition to more normal conditions of life. If things

[1] A pood is 36 pounds.

Peter Kropotkin in old age.

go on this way much longer, we are headed for a bloody catastrophe. Neither the locomotives of the Allies nor the export of grain, hemp, flax, leather and the like – things we need ourselves – can help the population.

One thing is certain. Even if a party dictatorship were the proper means to strike a blow at the capitalist system (which I strongly doubt), *it is positively harmful for the building of a new socialist system. What is needed is local construction by local forces.* Yet this is absent. It exists nowhere. Instead, wherever one turns there are people who have never known anything of real life committing the most flagrant errors, errors paid for in thousands of lives and in the devastation of whole regions.

Take, for instance, the procurement of wood or of seed for last spring's planting. Without the participation of local forces, without construction from below by the peasants and workers themselves, the building of a new life would be impossible.

Such construction from below, it would seem, would be best undertaken by the soviets. But Russia has already become a Soviet Republic only in name. The influx and bossism of party men, predominantly fledgeling Communists (the ideological old-timers are mainly in the larger centres), have already destroyed the influence and creative strength of these much-vaunted institutions, the soviets. At present it is not the soviets which rule in Russia but party committees. And their constructive ability suffers from all the inefficiencies of bureaucratic organization.

To escape from the existing dislocation, Russia must rely on the creativity of local forces, which, as I see it, can become a factor in the building of a new life. The sooner this is understood the better, and the more will people be inclined to adopt social forms of life.

If, however, the present situation is allowed to continue, the very word 'socialism' will become a curse, as happened in France with the idea of equality for forty years after the rule of the Jacobins.

With comradely greetings,
P. Kropotkin

Dmitrov, 4 March 1920

Dear Vladimir Ilyich,

Izvestia and *Pravda* have announced that the Soviet government has decided to take as hostages SRs from the Savinkov and Chernov groups, as well as White Guards of the National and Tactical Centre and Wrangelite officers,[1] and, in case of attempts on the lives of Soviet leaders, to execute these hostages 'without mercy'.

Is it possible that there is no one among you to remind and persuade his comrades that such measures constitute a return to the worst periods of the Middle Ages and religious wars? They are unworthy of men who have undertaken to build a future society on communal lines, and cannot be employed by those who hold dear the future of communism.

Is it possible that no one will explain the meaning of hostage?

A hostage is put in prison not as punishment for some crime. He is held, rather, to blackmail the enemy with his death: 'If you kill one of ours, we will kill one of yours.' But is this not the same as leading a man each morning to his execution and taking him back to jail, saying: 'Wait a bit . . . not today'?

Is it possible that your comrades do not understand that this is tantamount to *the revival of torture for the hostages and their families*?

I hope no one will tell me that life for men in power is not always easy. At present even among kings there are some who regard attempts on their lives as an 'occupational hazard'.

And revolutionaries in court – Louise Michel, for instance – undertake

---

[1] These anti-Bolshevik groups, ranging from the Socialist Revolutionary followers of Boris Savinkov and Victor Chernov through the Kadet National Centre to the military officers of General Wrangel, had all been dispersed by the autumn of 1920. Their leaders were in exile – Savinkov in Poland, Chernov in Czechoslovakia, Wrangel in Turkey – but many of the rank and file were languishing in Soviet prisons.

to defend their own would-be assassins, or they refuse, as did Malatesta and Voltairine de Cleyre, to press charges against them.[1]

Even kings and popes have rejected such barbarous means of defence as the taking of hostages. So how can the advocates of a new life and the builders of a new society resort to such a weapon of defence against their enemies?

Will this not be viewed as a sign that you already consider your communist experiment unsuccessful and are out to save your own necks?

Is it possible that your comrades do not realize that you, as communists, whatever mistakes you have made, are *working for the future* and hence must never tarnish your cause with acts resembling those of brute terror – that precisely such acts committed by revolutionaries of the past have made the new communist experiment so difficult?

I believe that, for the best among you, *the future of communism* is dearer than life itself, and that thoughts of this future will compel you to renounce such measures.

With all its great defects – and I, as you know, see them well – the October Revolution has brought about an enormous change. It has shown that a social revolution is not impossible, as they had begun to think in Western Europe. And, with all its defects, it will produce a change in the direction of *equality* which no efforts to return to the past will eliminate.

Why then push the revolution onto a road leading to its downfall, owing mainly to defects which have nothing in common with socialism or communism but which are survivals of the old order and old deformities, of unlimited and omnivorous authority?

P. Kropotkin

Dmitrov (Moscow Province)
21 December 1920

V. D. Bonch-Bruevich, 'Moi vospominaniia o Petre Alekseeviche Kropotkine', *Zvezda* (Leningrad), 1930, No. 6, pp. 182–211.

49 *Message to the Workers of the West* PETER KROPOTKIN

I have been asked whether I have not some message to send to the working men of the Western world? Surely there is much to say about the current events in Russia, and much to learn from them. The message might be long. But I shall indicate only some main points.

[1] Louise Michel, Errico Malatesta and Voltairine de Cleyre were prominent anarchists who were seriously wounded in unsuccessful assassination attempts in the late nineteenth and early twentieth centuries.

First of all, the working men of the civilised world and their friends in the other classes ought to induce their Governments entirely to abandon the idea of armed intervention in the affairs of Russia – whether open or disguised, whether military or in the shape of subventions to different nations.

Russia is now living through a Revolution of the same depth and the same importance as the British nation underwent in 1639–1648, and France in 1789–1794; and every nation should refuse to play the shameful part that Great Britain, Prussia, Austria and Russia played during the French Revolution.

Moreover, it must be kept in view that the Russian Revolution – while it is trying to build up a society where the whole produce of the joint efforts of Labour, technical skill, and scientific knowledge should go entirely to the Commonwealth itself – is not a mere accident in the struggle of Parties. It is something that has been prepared by nearly a century of Communist and Socialist propaganda, since the times of Robert Owen, Saint-Simon and Fourier; and although the attempt at introducing the new society by means of the dictatorship of one Party is apparently doomed to be a failure, it, nevertheless, must be recognised that the Revolution has already introduced into our everyday life new conceptions about the rights of Labour, its true position in Society, and the duties of every citizen, which have come to stay.

All concerned, not only the working men, but all of the progressive elements of the civilised nations, ought to put a stop to the support hitherto given to the opponents of the Revolution. Not that there should be nothing to oppose in the methods of the Bolshevist Government! Far from that. But because every armed intervention of a Foreign Power necessarily results in a reinforcement of the dictatorial tendencies of the rulers and paralyses the efforts of those Russians who are ready to aid Russia, independently of the Government, in the reconstruction of its life on new lines.

The evils, naturally inherent in Party Dictatorship, have thus been increased by the war conditions under which this Party maintained itself. The state of war has been an excuse for strengthening the dictatorial methods of the Party, as well as its tendency to centralise every detail of life in the hands of the Government; with the result that immense branches of the usual activities of the nation have been brought to a standstill. The natural evils of State Communism are thus increased tenfold under the excuse that all the misfortunes of our life are due to the intervention of the foreigners.

Besides, I must also mention that military intervention by the Allies, if it is continued, will certainly give rise in Russia to bitter feeling against the Western nations, and this will some day be utilised by their enemies in possible future conflicts. Such bitterness is already developing.

In short, it is high time that the West-European nations entered into direct relations with the Russian nation. And in this direction you – the working classes and the advanced portions of all nations – ought to have your say.

One more word about the general question. A renewal of relations between the European and American nations and Russia certainly must not mean the admission of a supremacy of the Russian nation over those nationalities of which the Empire of the Russian Tsars was composed. Imperial Russia is dead and will not return to life. The future of the various Provinces of which the Empire was composed lies in the direction of a great Federation. The natural territories of the different parts of that Federation are quite distinct for those of us who are acquainted with the history of Russia, its ethnography and its economic life; and all attempts to bring the constituent parts of the Russian Empire – Finland, the Baltic Provinces, Lithuania, the Ukraine, Georgia, Armenia, Siberia and so on – under one central rule are surely doomed to failure. The future of what was the Russian Empire is in the direction of a Federation of independent units.

It would therefore be in the interest of all that the Western nations should declare beforehand that they are recognising the right of self-government for every portion of what was once the Russian Empire.

As to my own views on the subject, they go still further. I see the coming in the near future of a time when every portion of that Federation will itself be a federation of free rural communes and free cities; and I still believe that portions of Western Europe will soon take the lead in that direction.

Now, as regards our present economical and political situation, the Russian Revolution being a continuation of the two great Revolutions, in England and in France, Russia is trying to make now a step in advance of where France stopped, when it came to realise in life what was described then as real equality (*égalité de fait*), that is, economic equality.

Unfortunately, the attempt to make that step has been undertaken in Russia under the strongly-centralised Dictatorship of one Party – the Social Democratic Maximalists [i.e., the Bolsheviks], and the attempt was made on the lines taken in the utterly Centralist and Jacobinist conspiracy of Babeuf. About this attempt I am bound frankly to tell you that, in my opinion, the attempt to build up a Communist Republic on the lines of strongly-centralised State-Communism, under the iron rule of the Dictatorship of a Party, is ending in a failure. We learn in Russia how Communism cannot be introduced, even though the populations, sick of the old regime, opposed no active resistance to the experiment made by the new rulers.

The idea of Soviets, that is, of Labour and Peasant Councils – first promoted during the attempted Revolution of 1905, and immediately realised by the Revolution of February, 1917, as soon as the Tsar's regime broke down – the idea of such Councils controlling the political and economic life of the country is a grand idea. The more so as it leads necessarily to the idea of those Councils being composed of all those who take a real part in the production of national wealth by their own personal effort.

But so long as a country is governed by the Dictatorship of a Party, the Labour and Peasant Councils evidently lose all their significance. They are reduced to the passive role played in times past by States-General and Parliaments, when they were convoked by the King and had to oppose an all-powerful King's Council.

A Labour Council ceases to be a free and valuable adviser when there is no free Press in the country; and we have been in this position for nearly two years – the excuse for such conditions being the state of war. More than that, the Peasant and Labour Councils lose all their significance when no free electoral agitation precedes the elections, and the elections are made under the pressure of Party Dictatorship. Of course, the usual excuse is that dictatorial rule was unavoidable as a means of combating the old regime. But such a rule evidently becomes a formidable drawback as soon as the Revolution proceeds towards the building-up of a new Society on a new economic basis; it becomes a death sentence on the new construction.

The ways to be followed in order to overthrow an already weakened Government and to take its place are well known from history, old and modern. But when it comes to the building-up of quite new forms of life – especially new forms of production and exchange, without having any examples to imitate; when everything has to be worked out by men on the spot; then an all-powerful centralised government which undertakes to supply every inhabitant with every lamp-glass and every match to light the lamp proves absolutely incapable of doing that through its functionaries, no matter how countless they may be; it becomes a nuisance. It develops such a formidable bureaucracy that the French bureaucratic system, which requires the intervention of forty functionaries to sell a tree felled by a storm on a *route nationale*, becomes a trifle in comparison. This is what we are now learning in Russia. And this is what you, the working men of the West, can and must avoid by all means, since you care for the success of a social reconstruction, and have sent your delegates here to see how a Social Revolution works in real life.

The immense constructive work that is required from a Social Revolution cannot be accomplished by a central government; even if it had, to guide it in its work, something more substantial than a few Socialist and Anarchist booklets. It requires the knowledge, the brains, and the willing collaboration of a mass of local and specialised forces, which alone can cope with the diversity of economic problems in their local aspects. To sweep away that collaboration and to trust to the genius of Party Dictators is to destroy all the independent nuclei, such as Trade Unions (called in Russia "Professional

The funeral of Kropotkin, 13 February 1921.

Unions") and the local Distributive Co-operative organisations – turning them into bureaucratic organs of the Party – as it is being done now. But this is the way *not* to accomplish the Revolution: the way to render its realisation impossible. And this is why I consider it my duty earnestly to warn you from taking such a line of action.

Imperialist conquerors of all nationalities may desire that the populations of the ex-Empire of Russia should remain in miserable economic conditions as long as possible, and thus be doomed to supply western and middle Europe with raw material; while the western manufacturers, producing manufactured goods, should cash all the benefits that the populations of Russia might otherwise obtain from their work. But the working classes of Europe and America, and the intellectual nuclei of these countries, surely understand that only by the force of conquest could they keep Russia in that subordinate condition. At the same time the sympathies with which our Revolution was met all over Europe and America show that you were happy to greet in Russia a new member of the international comradeship of nations. And you surely will soon see that it is in the interest of the workers of all the world that Russia should issue as soon as possible from the conditions that now paralyse her development.

A few words more. The last war has inaugurated new conditions of life in the civilised world. Socialism is sure to make considerable progress, and new forms of a more independent life surely will be soon worked out on

the lines of local political independence and free scope in social reconstruction, either in a pacific way, or by revolutionary means, if the intelligent
portions of the civilised nations do not join in the task of an unavoidable
reconstruction.

But the success of this reconstruction will depend to a great extent upon
the possibility of a close co-operation of the different nations. For this cooperation the labouring classes of all nations must be closely united; and
for that purpose the idea of a great International of all the working men of
the world must be renewed: not in the shape of a Union directed by one
single Party – as was the case in the Second International, and is again in the
Third. Such Unions have, of course, full reason to exist; but besides them,
and uniting them all, there must be a Union of all the Trade Unions of the
World – of all those who produce the wealth of the world, and united in
order to free the production of the world from its present enslavement to
Capital.

P. Kropotkin

Dmitrov, 10 June 1920

British Labour Delegation to Russia 1920: Report (London,
1920), 89-92, in English.

Starving children in Samara (modern Kuibyshev), October 1921.

Part Nine
Kronstadt

In March 1921 the sailors of the Kronstadt naval base in the Gulf of Finland near Petrograd rose in revolt against the Bolshevik government, which they themselves had helped into power. Under the slogan of 'free soviets', they established a revolutionary commune that survived for sixteen days, until an army was sent across the ice to crush it. After a long and savage struggle, with heavy losses on both sides, the rebels were subdued.

The Kronstadt rising was not, as is often alleged, inspired and led by anarchists – or, for that matter, by any other single party or group. Its participants were radicals of various types – SRs, Mensheviks, anarchists, rank-and-file Communists – who possessed no systematic ideology nor any carefully laid plan of action. Their credo (Documents 50, 51), compounded of elements from several revolutionary strains, was vague and ill-defined, more a list of grievances, an outcry of protest against misery and oppression, than a coherent revolutionary programme. In place of detailed proposals the insurgents preferred, in effect, to rely on what Kropotkin called 'the creative spirit of the masses', operating through freely elected soviets.

But if Kronstadt was not strictly speaking an anarchist affair, the spirit of anarchism, so powerful there during 1917, had by no means dissipated. One of the authors of the Petropavlovsk Resolution (Document 50), the political charter of the rebellion, was reputed to be an anarchist, and some of the key slogans of the movement – 'free soviets', 'third revolution', 'Down with the commissarocracy' (Document 51) – had been anarchist slogans during the Civil War, cropping up in (among other places) Gregory Maksimov's essay on the soviets (Document 29) and in the Makhno proclamations included above.

In any case, anarchists throughout Russia were elated by the rising. They hailed Kronstadt as 'the Second Paris Commune' and angrily denounced the government for sending troops against it. At the height of the insurrection, an anarchist leaflet appeared in the streets of Petrograd criticizing the population for turning its back on the rebels, for remaining silent while the thunder of artillery sounded in the Finnish Gulf (Document 52). Other anarchists, such as Alexander Berkman and Emma Goldman, sought to mediate the conflict and avert a bloodbath. But their efforts were in vain. The rebellion was mercilessly crushed, after which a new wave of political arrests swept the country. Anarchists were rounded up in Petrograd, Moscow, Kiev, Kharkov and other cities. In September 1921 the Cheka shot Fanya Baron and the anarchist poet Lev Cherny (see Document 53). Emma Goldman was so outraged that she had to be dissuaded by her comrades from chaining

The quelling of the Kronstadt rising. Red army units crossing the ice and (below) launching their attack on Kronstadt on the night of 17 March 1921.

herself to a bench in the hall where the Third International was meeting and shouting her protests to the delegates.

Amid protests at home and abroad, Lenin decided to release some of the better-known anarchist prisoners who had no record of violent opposition to the Soviet government. Maksimov, Volin and others departed for Berlin in January 1922. Meanwhile Alexander Berkman and Emma Goldman, disheartened and disillusioned, decided to leave also (Document 53). Those who remained were rejected, reviled, and finally stamped out or driven into exile. Yet, though they suffered the melancholy of defeat, the anarchists retained their idealism to the end and clung to the hope that ultimately their vision of a stateless society would triumph. 'Bolshevism is of the past', wrote Berkman in the early 1920s, when his comrades were in prison or exile. 'The future belongs to man and his liberty.'

50 *The* Petropavlovsk *Resolution*

Having heard the report of the representatives sent by the general meeting of ships' crews to Petrograd to investigate the situation there, we resolve:

1 In view of the fact that the present soviets do not express the will of the workers and peasants, immediately to hold new elections by secret ballot, with freedom to carry on agitation beforehand for all workers and peasants;

2 To give freedom of speech and press to workers and peasants, to anarchists and left socialist parties;

3 To secure freedom of assembly for trade unions and peasant organizations;

4 To call a non-party conference of the workers, Red Army soldiers and sailors of Petrograd, Kronstadt and Petrograd province, no later than 10 March 1921;

5 To liberate all political prisoners of socialist parties, as well as all workers, peasants, soldiers and sailors imprisoned in connection with the labour and peasant movements;

6 To elect a commission to review the cases of those being held in prisons and concentration camps;

7 To abolish all political departments, since no party should be given special privileges in the propagation of its ideas or receive the financial support of the state for such purposes. Instead cultural and educational commissions should be established, locally elected and financed by the state;

8 To remove all road-block detachments immediately;[1]

9 To equalize the rations of all working people, with the exception of those employed in trades detrimental to health;

[1] Armed squads which confiscated food illegally purchased by city dwellers from the peasantry.

10 To abolish the Communist fighting detachments in all branches of the army, as well as the Communist guards kept on duty in factories and mills. Should such guards or detachments be found necessary, they are to be appointed in the army from the ranks and in the factories and mills at the discretion of the workers;

11 To give the peasants full freedom of action in regard to the land, and also the right to keep cattle, on condition that the peasants manage with their own means, that is, without employing hired labour;

12 To request all branches of the army, as well as our comrades the military cadets, to endorse our resolution;

13 To demand that the press give all our resolutions wide publicity;

14 To appoint an itinerant bureau of control;

15 To permit free handicrafts production by one's own labour.

> PETRICHENKO, Chairman of the Squadron Meeting
> PEREPELKIN, Secretary

Pravda o Kronshtadte (Prague, 1921), 46–7.

51 *What We Are Fighting For*

After carrying out the October Revolution, the working class had hoped to achieve its emancipation. But the result was an even greater enslavement of the human personality. The power of the police and gendarme monarchy passed into the hands of the Communist usurpers, who, instead of giving the people freedom, instilled in them the constant fear of falling into the torture chambers of the Cheka, which in their horrors far exceed the gendarme administration of the tsarist regime. The bayonets, bullets and gruff commands of the Cheka *oprichniki*[1] – these are what the working man of Soviet Russia has won after so much struggle and suffering. The glorious emblem of the workers' state – the sickle and hammer – has in fact been replaced by the Communist authorities with the bayonet and barred window, for the sake of maintaining the calm and carefree life of the new bureaucracy of Communist commissars and functionaries.

But most infamous and criminal of all is the moral servitude which the Communists have inaugurated: they have laid their hands also on the inner world of the toilers, forcing them to think in the Communist way. With the help of the bureaucratized trade unions they have fastened the workers to their benches, so that labour has become not a joy but a new form of slavery. To the protests of the peasants, expressed in spontaneous uprisings, and those of the workers, whose living conditions have driven them out on strike, they reply with mass executions and bloodletting, in which they

[1] Ivan the Terrible's secret police, who conducted a bloody reign of terror in the sixteenth century.

have not been surpassed even by the tsarist generals. Russia of the toilers, the first to raise the red banner of labour's emancipation, is drenched in the blood of those martyred for the glory of Communist domination. In this sea of blood, the Communists are drowning all the great and glowing pledges and watchwords of the workers' revolution. The picture has been drawn more and more sharply, and now it is clear that the Russian Communist party is not the defender of the toilers that it pretends to be. The interests of the working people are alien to it. Having gained power, it is afraid only of losing it, and therefore deems every means permissible: slander, violence, deceit, murder, vengeance upon the families of the rebels.[1]

The long-suffering patience of the toilers is at an end. Here and there the land is lit by the fires of insurrection in a struggle against oppression and violence. Strikes by the workers have flared up, but the Bolshevik *okhrana*[2] agents have not been asleep and have taken every measure to forestall and suppress the inevitable third revolution. But it has come nevertheless, and it is being made by the hands of the toilers themselves. The generals of Communism see clearly that it is the people who have risen, convinced that the ideas of socialism have been betrayed. Yet trembling for their skins and aware that there is no escape from the wrath of the workers they still try, with the help of their *oprichniki*, to terrorize the rebels with prison, firing-squads and other atrocities. But life under the yoke of the Communist dictatorship has become more terrible than death.

The rebellious working people understand that there is no middle ground in the struggle against the Communists and the new serfdom that they have erected. One must go on to the end. They give the appearance of making concessions: in Petrograd province road-block detachments have been removed and ten million gold roubles has been allotted for the purchase of foodstuffs from abroad. But one must not be deceived, for behind this bait is concealed the iron hand of the master, the dictator, who aims to be repaid a hundredfold for his concessions once calm is restored.

No, there can be no middle ground. Victory or death! The example is being set by Red Kronstadt, scourge of counter-revolutionaries of the Right and of the Left. Here the new revolutionary step forward has been taken. Here is raised the banner of rebellion against the three-year-old violence and oppression of Communist rule, which has put in the shade the three-hundred-year yoke of monarchism. Here in Kronstadt has been laid the first stone of the third revolution, striking the last fetters from the labouring masses and opening a broad new road for socialist creativity.

This new revolution will also rouse the labouring masses of the East and

---

[1] The last phrase refers to the seizure of the rebels' families as hostages.
[2] The tsarist secret police, forerunner of the Cheka.

160

of the West, by serving as an example of the new socialist construction as opposed to bureaucratic Communist 'creativity'. The labouring masses abroad will see with their own eyes that everything hitherto created here by the will of the workers and peasants was not socialism. Without a single shot, without a drop of blood, the first step has been taken. The toilers do not need blood. They will shed it only in a moment of self-defence. In spite of all the outrageous acts of the Communists, we have enough restraint to confine ourselves only to isolating them from public life so that their malicious and false agitation will not hinder our revolutionary work.

The workers and peasants steadfastly march forward, leaving behind them the Constituent Assembly, with its bourgeois regime, and the dictatorship of the Communist party, with its Cheka and its state capitalism, whose hangman's noose encircles the necks of the labouring masses and threatens to strangle them to death. The present upheaval at last gives the toilers the opportunity to have their freely elected soviets, operating without the slightest force of party pressure, and to remake the bureaucratized trade unions into free associations of workers, peasants and the labouring intelligentsia. At last the policeman's club of the Communist autocracy has been broken.

'Za chto my boremsia', *Izvestiia Vremennogo Revoliutsionnogo Komiteta*, 8 March 1921, in *Pravda o Kronshtadte*, 82–4.

52 *Where There is Authority There is No Freedom*

What is taking place in Kronstadt – a revolution or a counter-revolution, a rising for freedom or a White Guard mutiny? 'White mutiny and counter-revolution,' declare its Soviet enemies. 'The Kronstadters have risen against us. They have departed from our path. And their new path leads only to the camp of the Whites, to the camp of counter-revolution. There is no other exit.'

But we anarchists say: there are two paths, quite different ones. One leads to authority, the other away from it. In this respect both the Soviet government and the White Guards march together. Monarchists, Constituent Assemblists, Mensheviks, Communists – when they have the same means and the same ends can their paths be different? They want to recruit more members into their parties. They want strong authority. But strong authority implies subjection. This in turn requires iron discipline and a compulsory army. It's easy to rule when the people are downtrodden and exhausted. For the peasants this means the requisitioning of grain, for the workers forced labour. And such authority will not shrink even from concessions to foreigners by selling the labour as well as the freedom of the workers, if by such means it can strengthen its own power. Thus Lenin says at the Tenth Party Congress: 'We must adapt our economy, now geared to the tasks of war, to the tasks of peaceful construction, with concessions at the top and taxes below. We cannot, of course, manage now without compulsion, for the country is impoverished and exhausted.' Such is the path of the Communists, and such is the only path for all holders of authority. If the Kronstadters were to follow this path, it would mean that they were for authority and that their rising was counter-revolutionary.

About the second path they remain silent. All governments consciously conceal it, for it means the death of all authority. It is, in short, the absence of power. Here there are no commanders, which means that there are no slaves, no labour armies, no labour conscription, no compulsion. Each man, rather, works for his own life. In place of a compulsory army there are free partisan detachments. In place of compulsory labour there is free labour. The production and distribution of goods is managed by the workers themselves. Without the aid of authority they carry on free exchange with the peasants. The solution of economic problems takes place at free factory committee and peasant meetings.

The freedom-loving Kronstadters do not desire the cudgel. They have risen against authority. The Kronstadt rising is a revolution.

And yet you men of Petrograd remain silent and fail to act. The revolution has long been awaiting you. It calls to you from Kronstadt. For several days you have wavered. You have not grasped the whole truth of events. The Soviet government has maliciously deceived you in order to save its own skin. In order to survive it thinks it necessary to defeat Kronstadt. But who would murder sailors to defend authority? So they have made up some trite old story about a counter-revolution. They wanted to deceive Petrograd. They wanted to deceive Russia again. But whoever knew Kronstadt knew its love of freedom and could not believe that the sailors were conspiring with the *Entente*. Only a part of our inexperienced youth, flattered by the title of 'brave defenders of Petrograd', could swallow this story. Led by experienced scoundrels, they began to threaten the revolution with shells. Here is the truth about those days. Yet knowing the truth you Petrograders still remain silent. Night and day you hear the rumble of cannon and yet fail to come out openly against the government and thereby deflect its forces away from Kronstadt. Don't you see that the cause of Kronstadt is your cause? You, no less than the Kronstadters, have been tormented by the Soviet government these three years. Little by little it has killed in you all that once was alive, killed every thought, every hope in the possibility of a new revolution, even in the remote possibility of liberation.

The Kronstadters have always been the first to rise. And now they are again the first to free their throats from the strangler's grip. As a result, we can see in the distance, from Kronstadt, amid the thunder of cannon, the signal flashes of freedom.

Now it's your turn. Let the Kronstadt revolt be followed by a Petrograd revolt. Sailors, soldiers, workers – arise together with Kronstadt. Let the government march against you with its bands of military cadets. Then we shall see which of us will be favoured by victory and the revolution. People of Petrograd, your first task is to destroy this government. Your second is not to create any other. For every authority brings with it, on the very first day, laws and restrictions.

Only with the absence of authority will there be no one above you. And now vessels, factories, military units – join together. Discuss and arrange your common action. Advance in collectives in every area with every weapon. The government will meet you with bullets. It is thus that every authority meets the revolution. But as always it will be its swansong. Let anarchy follow you in triumph!

The Anarchists

'Gde vlast' – tam net svobody', in N. A. Kornatovskii, ed., *Kronshtadtskii miatezh* (Leningrad, 1931), 164–6.

53 The Bolshevik Myth   ALEXANDER BERKMAN

7 March – Distant rumbling reaches my ears as I cross the Nevsky.[1] It sounds again, stronger and nearer, as if rolling toward me. All at once I realize that artillery is being fired. It is 6 p.m. Kronstadt has been attacked!

Days of anguish and cannonading. My heart is numb with despair; something has died within me. The people on the streets look bowed with grief, bewildered. No one trusts himself to speak. The thunder of heavy guns rends the air.

17 March – Kronstadt has fallen today.

Thousands of sailors and workers lie dead in its streets. Summary execution of prisoners and hostages continues.

18 March – The victors are celebrating the anniversary of the Commune of 1871. Trotsky and Zinoviev denounce Thiers and Gallifet for the slaughter of the Paris rebels. . . .[2]

17 September – At noon today the hunger strikers were released from the Taganka,[3] two months after the Government had pledged their liberation. The men look worn and old, withered by anguish and privation. They

---

[1] The Nevsky Prospect, the main avenue of Petrograd.

[2] Thiers was premier of France and Gallifet the general who subdued the Paris Communards.

[3] In July 1921 several prominent anarchists in Moscow's Taganka prison – among them Volin and Maksimov – staged an eleven-day hunger strike to protest their confinement. They were eventually released and deported to Germany in January 1922.

have been put under surveillance and forbidden to meet their comrades. It is said weeks will pass before opportunity will be given them to leave the country. They are not permitted to work and they have no means of subsistence. The Cheka declares that no other politicals will be freed. Arrests of revolutionists are taking place throughout the country.

30 September – With bowed heart I seek a familiar bench in the park. Here little Fanya sat at my side. Her face was turned to the sun, her whole being radiant with idealism. Her silvery laughter rang with the joy of youth and life, but I trembled for her safety at every approaching step. "Do not fear," she kept reassuring me, "no one will know me in my peasant disguise."

Now she is dead. Executed yesterday by the Cheka as a "bandit".

Gray are the passing days. One by one the embers of hope have died out. Terror and despotism have crushed the life born in October. The slogans of the Revolution are foresworn, its ideals stifled in the blood of the people. The breath of yesterday is dooming millions to death; the shadow of today hangs like a black pall over the country. Dictatorship is trampling the masses under foot. The Revolution is dead; its spirit cries in the wilderness.

High time the truth about the Bolsheviki were told. The whited sepulcher must be unmasked, the clay feet of the fetish beguiling the international proletariat to fatal will o' the wisps exposed. The Bolshevik myth must be destroyed.

I have decided to leave Russia.

Alexander Berkman, *The Bolshevik Myth (Diary 1920–1922)* (New York, 1925), 303, 318–19.

Alexander Berkman.

Emma Goldman.

54 *My Disillusionment in Russia* EMMA GOLDMAN

The libertarian principle was strong in the initial days of the Revolution, the need for free expression all-absorbing. But when the first wave of enthusiasm receded into the ebb of everyday prosaic life, a firm conviction was needed to keep the fires of liberty burning. There was only a comparative handful in the great vastness of Russia to keep those fires lit – the Anarchists, whose number was small and whose efforts, absolutely suppressed under the Tsar, had had no time to bear fruit. The Russian people, to some extent instinctive Anarchists, were yet too unfamiliar with true libertarian principles and methods to apply them effectively to life. Most of the Russian Anarchists themselves were unfortunately still in the meshes of limited group activities and of individualistic endeavour as against the more important social and collective efforts. The Anarchists, the future unbiassed historian will admit, have played a very important role in the Russian Revolution – a role far more significant and fruitful than their comparatively small number would have led one to expect. Yet honesty and sincerity compel me to state that their work would have been of infinitely greater practical value had they been better organized and equipped to guide the released energies of the people towards the re-organization of life on a libertarian foundation.

But the failure of the Anarchists in the Russian Revolution – in the sense just indicated – does by no means argue the defeat of the libertarian idea. On the contrary, the Russian Revolution has demonstrated beyond doubt that the State idea, State Socialism, in all its manifestations (economic, 165 political, social, educational) is entirely and hopelessly bankrupt. Never before in all history has authority, government, the State, proved so inherently static, reactionary, and even counter-revolutionary in effect. In short, the very antithesis of revolution.

It remains true as it has through all progress, that only the libertarian spirit and method can bring man a step further in his eternal striving for the better, finer, and freer life. Applied to the great social upheavals known as revolutions, this tendency is as potent as in the ordinary evolutionary process. The authoritarian method has been a failure all through history and now it has again failed in the Russian Revolution. So far human ingenuity has discovered no other principle except the libertarian, for man has indeed uttered the highest wisdom when he said that liberty is the mother of order, not its daughter.[1] All political tenets and parties notwithstanding, no revolution can be truly and permanently successful unless it puts its emphatic veto upon all tyranny and centralization, and determinedly strives to make the revolution a real revaluation of all economic, social, and cultural values.[2] Not mere substitution of one political party for another in the control of the Government, not the masking of autocracy by proletarian slogans, not the dictatorship of a new class over an old one, not political scene shifting of any kind, but the complete reversal of all these authoritarian principles will alone serve the revolution.

Emma Goldman, *My Disillusionment in Russia* (London, 1925), 251–3.

---

[1] A famous dictum of Proudhon's.

[2] 'Revaluation of all values': a phrase of Nietzsche's, a thinker whom Emma greatly admired.

*The victors of Kronstadt. Lenin (standing, front row, right) with
Communist Party delegates just after the mutiny had been put down.*

Stepan Maksimovich Petrichenko, one of the leaders of the Kronstadt revolt and co-author of the Petropavlovsk Resolution *(see pp. 158–9), arrives on Finnish soil after the failure of the rising.*

Bibliographical Note

There is an extensive literature on Russian anarchism during the Revolution and Civil War. The following note mentions only the most important works on the subject. For a full annotated bibliography see Paul Avrich, *The Russian Anarchists* (Princeton, 1967), 259–89.

General Works on Anarchism: Over the past decade a spate of new books has appeared dealing with the history of anarchist ideas and movements. Of these works George Woodcock's *Anarchism* (Cleveland, 1962) is the most comprehensive general history and the best introduction to the subject. *The Anarchists* by James Joll (London, 1964) offers a stimulating interpretative account with a brief discussion of the Russian Revolution. A good short work, with an interesting chapter on the Russian Revolution, is Daniel Guérin's *Anarchism* (New York, 1970), which originally appeared in French in 1965. Guérin has also put together a handsome anarchist anthology, with material on Makhno and Kronstadt, entitled *Ni Dieu ni maître* (Paris, 1965). As a concise, up-to-date analysis of what anarchists believe and how they act, Nicolas Walter's pamphlet *About Anarchism* (London, 1969, with many translations) has no equal.

Anarchism in the Russian Revolution: *The Origin of the Communist Autocracy* by Leonard Shapiro (London, 1955) is an outstanding history of political opposition to the Bolshevik regime, including a brief but valuable section on the anarchists. *The Russian Anarchists* by Paul Avrich (Princeton, 1967) presents the fullest scholarly account in English. Among the participants themselves, two of the most prominent, Volin and Maksimov, have left detailed works of exceptional value. *La Révolution inconnue (1917–1921)* by Volin (V. M. Eikhenbaum) (Paris, 1947; reprinted 1969) is an indispensable first-hand account, a large portion of which has been translated into English by Holley Cantine and published in two volumes entitled *Nineteen-Seventeen* and *The Unknown Revolution* (London and New York, 1954–55). G. P. Maksimov's *The Guillotine at Work* (Chicago, 1940) presents a severe indictment of the suppression of the anarchists, with a wealth of supporting documents.

Other well-known anarchists also have left valuable memoirs of the period. Emma Goldman's *Living My Life* (2 vols., New York, 1931) is a memorable autobiography containing a good deal of material on the anarchists in the Revolution. It has recently been reprinted in an attractive paperback edition by Dover Publications (New York, 1970). For further reminiscences see her *My Disillusionment in Russia* (London, 1925), reissued in paper covers by Apollo Editions (New York, 1970). Richard Drinnon's *Rebel in Paradise* (Chicago, 1961) is a fine biography of Emma which discusses her activities in Russia during the Civil War period. *The Bolshevik Myth* (New York, 1925) is an absorbing diary by Emma's fellow militant and long-time companion, Alexander Berkman. The concluding chapter was published separately under the title *The "Anti-Climax"* (Berlin, 1925). Another essential source, by a former anarchist turned Bolshevik, is Victor Serge's *Memoirs of a Revolutionary, 1901–1941*, translated from the French by Peter Sedgwick (London, 1963).

The voluminous writings of Peter Kropotkin, the most celebrated of the Russian anarchists, are available for the most part in English. Nearly all of his major works – *Mutual Aid, The Conquest of Bread, Fields, Factories and Workshops, Ethics* – have been recently reprinted, and Nicolas Walter is now engaged in preparing the first full English translation of his *Words of a Rebel*. A good collection of his shorter pieces, including selections from the revolutionary period, is *Kropotkin's Revolutionary Pamphlets* (New York, 1927), edited by Roger N. Baldwin and reprinted in paper covers by Dover in 1970. For a recent appraisal of Kropotkin's influence and of his role in the Russian Revolution see my introductions to the Penguin editions of *Mutual Aid* and *The Conquest of Bread* (London, 1972).

A few works in Russian are of central importance and thus deserve mention. *Mikhailu Bakuninu, 1876–1926* [To Michael Bakunin, 1876–1926], edited by A. A. Borovoi (Moscow, 1926), and *P. A. Kropotkin i ego uchenie* [P. A. Kropotkin and His Teachings], edited by G. P. Maksimov (Chicago, 1931), are indispensable collections of articles and reminiscences written and compiled by leading participants in the movement. In addition, *Goneniia na anarkhizm v Sovetskoi Rossii* [The Persecution of the Anarchists in Soviet Russia] (Berlin, 1922, translated into French and German) is a major source on the suppression of the anarchists after 1917, with brief biographies of many of the best-known figures.

Makhno: Makhno's personal recollections of his guerrilla exploits in the Revolution and Civil War were published in three volumes (Paris, 1929–37) entitled *Russkaia revoliutsiia na Ukraine* [The Russian Revolution in the Ukraine], *Pod udarami kontr-revoliutsii* [Under the Blows of the Counter-revolution] and *Ukrainskaia revoliutsiia* [The Ukrainian Revolution]. Volume I has been translated into French (Paris, 1929), and a full French edition is now in preparation. *Istoriia makhnovskogo dvizheniia (1918–1921 gg.)* [A History of the Makhno Movement, 1918–1921] by Peter Arshinov (Berlin, 1923) is the most valuable history in Russian, written by one of

Makhno's closest associates. It has appeared in several translations, including French and German, and a new French edition was published in Paris in 1969. The best account in English is Chapter VI of David Footman's *Civil War in Russia* (London, 1961), originally published in *St. Antony's Papers*, No. 6 (London, 1959), pp. 75–127. In addition, *Apostles of Revolution* by Max Nomad (Boston, 1939) has an interesting chapter on Makhno which, unfortunately, has been omitted from the paperback edition brought out by Collier Books (New York, 1961).

Kronstadt: The most important source is *Pravda o Kronshtadte* [The Truth About Kronstadt] (Prague, 1921), which contains all fourteen issues of the rebel daily newspaper (recently translated into German and French). The fullest history of the revolt is *Kronstadt 1921* by Paul Avrich (Princeton, 1970). George Katkov's 'The Kronstadt Rising', *St. Antony's Papers*, No. 6 (London, 1959), pp. 9–74, provides an intelligent analysis. A well-informed, sensitive history of the rising from an anarchist perspective is *La Commune de Cronstadt* by Ida Mett (2nd edn, Paris, 1949). A slightly abridged English translation was published by the Solidarity Press (London, 1967). Alexander Berkman's *The Kronstadt Rebellion* (Berlin, 1922) is a briefer but equally perceptive anarchist account. Finally, of interest for both Makhno and Kronstadt is Ugo Fedeli's *Dalla insurrezione dei contadini in Ucraina alla rivolta di Cronstadt* (Milan, 1950).

Chronology

1876	*1 July*	Death of Bakunin
1905	*9 January*	'Bloody Sunday'
	13 October	Formation of Petersburg Soviet
	6–17 December	Moscow uprising
1906	*July*	*Burevestnik* founded in Paris
	September	Formation of South Russian Group of Anarcho-Syndicalists
		Arrests and trials of anarchists
1907	*August*	International Congress of Anarchists in Amsterdam
1911		*Golos Truda* founded in New York
		First signs of anarchist revival in Russia
1914	*1 August*	First World War begins
		Debates between 'defencist' and anti-militarist anarchists
1917	*February*	February Revolution
	March	Amnesty of political prisoners
	2 March	Abdication of the tsar; formation of Provisional Government
		Formation of Petrograd and Moscow Federations of Anarchist-Communist Groups
	June	Kropotkin returns to Russia
		Durnovo *dacha* confiscated by anarchists
	3–5 July	'July Days'
	18–22 July	Conference of anarchists in Kharkov
	August	*Golos Truda* re-established in Petrograd
	24–28 August	Kornilov affair
	October	Formation of Military-Revolutionary Committee with four anarchist members
	17–22 October	All-Russian Conference of Factory Committees
	25 October	October Revolution

	14 November	Decree on workers' control
1918	*6 January*	Dissolution of Constituent Assembly
	3 March	Treaty of Brest-Litovsk
	12 March	Government moved from Petrograd to Moscow
	11–12 April	Cheka raids on Moscow anarchists
	25 August–1 September	First All-Russian Conference of Anarcho-Syndicalists
	12–16 November	First Conference of *Nabat* Confederation
	25 November–1 December	Second All-Russian Congress of Anarcho-Syndicalists
	25 December	All-Russian Congress of Anarchist-Communists
1919	*23 January*	First Regional Congress of Peasants, Workers and Insurgents (Makhnovists)
	12 February	Second Regional Conference of Peasants, Workers and Insurgents
	2–7 April	First Congress of *Nabat* Confederation
	10 April	Third Regional Congress of Peasants, Workers and Insurgents
	25 September	Underground anarchists bomb Communist headquarters in Moscow
	26 September	Makhno routs Denikin's forces at Peregonovka
1920	*26 November*	Communist raids on Makhno's headquarters at Gulyai-Polye; arrest of *Nabat* Confederation
1921	*8 February*	Death of Kropotkin
	13 February	Funeral of Kropotkin
	1–18 March	Kronstadt uprising; suppression of anarchists in Russia
1922	*January*	Group of anarchist leaders deported from Russia
1929		Arrest of surviving anarchists in Russia
1934		Death of Makhno in Paris
1935–38		Stalin's purges
1936		Suicide of Berkman in Nice
1939		Kropotkin Museum closed
1940		Death of Emma Goldman in Toronto
1945		Death of Volin in Paris
1946		Death of Shapiro in New York
1950		Death of Maksimov in Chicago

Sources of Illustrations

New York Public Library frontispiece, pp. 67, 129 (*top*); Roger-Viollet p. 8; Novosti pp. 11 (*top*), 13, 15, 31, 123, 157 (*both*), 167; Mansell pp. 29, 53; Radio Times Hulton Picture Library pp. 32 (*right*), 79, 97, 107, 139 (*top*), 155; Courtesy Senya Fleshin p. 32 (*left*); Hoover Library pp. 39, 81, 127 (*bottom*); Imperial War Museum p. 43; Courtesy Boris Yelensky p. 57; Victoria and Albert Museum p. 69 (*bottom*); Illustration pp. 83, 168; Courtesy F. Rocker p. 88; *Illustrated London News* p. 139 (*bottom*); Bund Archive p. 147; Instituut voor Soc. Geschiedenis p. 164.

Index

DATE DUE

1-15-75			
OCT 6 1977			
GAYLORD			PRINTED IN U.S.A.